Sport and the English Countryside:
The World of John Moore

SPORT & THE ENGLISH COUNTRYSIDE

THE WORLD OF JOHN MOORE

Selected and Introduced by
DAPHNE MOORE

Foreword by PHIL DRABBLE

·THE·
SPORTSMAN'S
PRESS
LONDON

Published by The Sportsman's Press, 1987

© Extracts from John Moore's writing: Lucile Bell, 1987
© The introduction and linking passages: Daphne Moore, 1987

All rights reserved. No part of this publication may be reproduced, stored in a retrieval system, or transmitted in any form or by any means, electronic, mechanical, photocopying, recording or otherwise, without the prior permission of the publishers.

British Library Cataloguing in Publication Data

Moore, John, *1907–1967*
Sport and the English countryside: the world of John Moore.
1. Hunting 2. Sports
I. Title II. Moore, Daphne
799   SK31

ISBN 0-948253-18-5

Printed in Great Britain by
Adlard & Son Ltd, The Garden City Press, Dorking, Surrey

For Lucile,
with love

Contents

Acknowledgements	8
Foreword	9
John Moore	11
Prologue	23
Fishing	41
Shooting	75
Hunting	103
Country Life	131
Horses	159
Conservation	181
Weather	195
Epilogue	205

Acknowledgements

My grateful thanks are due to all those who have helped me in the creation of this anthology: to my sister-in-law, Lucile for supplying the photographs and assisting in numerous other ways; to Michael Pinker for his continuing and unswerving encouragement and helpfulness; to Stephen Walker who efficiently produced all the photocopies of the selected extracts, and to his wife, Janice, for deciphering my manuscript pages and putting them in type.

I would also like to acknowlege the use of an article published in *Blackwood's Magazine* of March 1978, which forms part of my introduction.

Thanks are also due to the following for permission to reproduce illustrations:

A. R. Bell (the modern photographs of High Street and Church Street, Tewkesbury)
Elliott & Fry Ltd (John Moore in 1944)
Clayton Evans (John Moore with Candy)
Ben Hooper (Lower Mill Farm)
Eric Wynter (Tewkesbury Abbey)

DAPHNE MOORE

Foreword by Phil Drabble

John Moore belonged to what is now an endangered species of 'Sportsman–Naturalist'. He loved fishing and shooting and, as a boy, he was an avid collector of butterflies, all of which are frowned on by fashionable conservationists today!

But nobody was a truer countryman or loved the countryside more deeply. He realised that the glorious patchwork of little fields and woodland owed their origin to the men who had created and maintained uneconomic copses and spinneys as cover for pheasants and foxes.

He realised too that there is room, in the countryside, for an almost infinite variety of interests, *provided* that there is plenty of give and take!

I first met him forty years ago as a fellow contributor to the radio programme 'Countrylover', which was presented by the late Freddie Grisewood. He was recalling his experiences as a fisherman and I was talking about ratting, with ferrets and my beloved Stafford bull terriers. We hit it off immediately and, thereafter, our paths did not simply cross at frequent intervals but ran absolutely parallel.

One radio programme we both enjoyed enormously was called 'Sunday Out'. A team of four people with differing interests was sent out on Friday night to stay in some village pub, get to know the locals and share their fun on Saturday so that a producer and recording car could come out on Sunday and make a programme about what we had been doing.

Geoffrey Bright, a distinguished estate agent would 'cover' the local Big House or church or tradition, I was the chap who walked with his dog and John described the attractions of the area, as seen from the back of a horse!

He had a marvellous way with words and could breathe life into the countryside with an apparently casual throwaway line. A programme we did one spring near Bridgnorth has always stuck in my mind. The whole skyline was white with damson blossom and lesser men would have fallen for the temptation to romanticise the scene. John brought it down to earth by reminding us of autumn, when the same trees 'would be laden with bitter bellyaching fruit!'

His writing was as vivid as his broadcasting – and less transient and his sister has chosen a magnum of her favourite extracts for this book.

My own path crossed with his again because he contributed the weekly country column for the *Birmingham Evening Mail* for eighteen years until within a fortnight of his death in 1967 and I have done a weekly column for the same paper since 1964 – and I still get letters from readers who remember him with great affection.

His voice fired the warning shots about the dangers of poisonous chemicals on the land and he waged verbal war on landowners in his area who were persecuting badgers decades before the modern scourge of badger baiting started.

This book gives a delightful taste of the magic of John Moore's country writing and the works into which Daphne Moore has dipped will be counted among the really great rural writing of our time.

JOHN MOORE

When my brother John died in 1967, Sir Compton Mackenzie wrote of him in *The Times:* 'The death of John Moore is a tragedy not only for those who mourn the loss of a dearly loved friend; it is also a tragedy for the English countryside. No writer, in these days when the English countryside is being slowly exterminated to gratify material progress, was able to preserve what life is left to it with the eloquent and accurate observation of John Moore. And now he has gone, gone with the Adonis blues and silver-washed fritillaries, gone with the brown squirrels and the birds of once upon a time. In my personal grief I think of him in the Elysian fields with Gilbert White and Jefferies and Cobbett talking of that countryside.'

It is never easy to write a biography of a close relation, and to write dispassionately of a much-loved brother is almost an impossibility. His books, of which there were an incredible 40 or more, gave a truer picture of the man than it is possible to paint in this introduction, but there are aspects of him which can only be revealed by someone who knew him from childhood.

My earliest recollections are of our life in Tudor House, Tewkesbury, of which John wrote so affectionately in his book, *Portrait of Elmbury*. We went to live there when I was only a few months old and John himself nearing his third birthday. It was an enchanting house for children, with queer old attics and a day-nursery which was panelled in old oak, and which had deep window-seats from which we could look out on to the main street and watch all the dramas which were enacted there; in those days Tewkesbury was a backwater, with traffic at a minimum and that principally horse-drawn. In the gutter of what is now a busy thoroughfare little boys played marbles, there were Punch and Judy Shows and many a barrel organ with the organ-grinder's monkey dressed up in a miniature suit, seated on top. Once, on a never-to-be-forgotten occasion, I actually saw a dancing bear in the main street, walking upright beside its master. It was, I suppose, a brown bear; probably the last of its kind ever to be seen in Tewkesbury.

This, then, was the town of our childhood, and though we lived in a town, we were country children, for the countryside was almost on our doorstep and less than five minutes' walk would bring us to the river. Tewkesbury was a place dominated first and foremost by its glorious Norman Abbey, and secondly by the two rivers, the Avon and Severn, whose waters converged on the very edge of the town itself. It was an easy walk across the Ham, the vast river-meadow completely surrounded by water, which John described as the 'town's playground', and when our legs were long enough to take us thus far, we derived great joy from going 'elvering' at the weir. Here the Severn waters tumbled in a huge, frothy, foamy torrent and the thread-like young eels were easy to catch in the still waters and little pools below. I can still smell that 'unforgettable, unforgotten river smell' which also seemed to carry with it something of the tang of the sea. We were never allowed to eat the fruit of our labours, but they were fried up with egg and breadcrumbs for the delectation of the kitchen staff, and the aroma was so appetising, that, forgetting their original slimy state, we longed for a taste of that forbidden feast.

There were river picnics, too, when John and I fished earnestly from a rowing boat with rod and line, but caught little but eels and the occasional roach.

John's literary tendencies were manifested at a very early age. At about twelve years old he was compiling *Moore's Natural History*, in several volumes. Written on loose sheets of paper and painstakingly sewn into brown paper covers, they included learned observations on birds, animals and flowers, and were illustrated with pencil drawings. When we were very young and were taken for walks by our current nanny or nursery governess, he showed his predilection for writing by tracing letters in the air with his forefinger as he strode along. We used to call him 'Johnny-head-in-air' from the verses in *Struwwelpeter*, a book which, with its tragic warnings and alarming pictures, I abominated. He was also nicknamed 'The Professor' by some of our Tewkesbury friends, for he was always a dedicated observer of nature, and would skin and dissect small mammals, set butterflies and moths with exquisite delicacy and precision, and was remarkably well-informed about all matters concerning the countryside.

He had been born just outside Tewkesbury, at a charming Georgian house standing on its own little hillock, named Uplands. This had been taken by my father on a short lease prior to moving into Tudor House, and subsequently, by a curious coincidence, we moved back there for the summer of 1917. Since it was wartime, this was presumably in lieu of a summer holiday, for the house was rented from its wealthy owner for a period of six months, and it proved to be a happy thought, for nowhere could have given us greater joy. As if in compensation for the last summer of a way of life to which we, as children, had become accustomed – with a loving father, security, and apparently ample means – everything about that 1917 summer was touched with magic. Even now I can feel the magic, and those brief months stand out in my memory as something belonging almost to another world. The weather was phenomenal, fine and hot day after day, and there was so much to be explored, so much to be experienced. The extraordinary invasion of Comma butterflies was in itself memorable (and I never see a comparatively rare Comma today without remembering that host of winged invaders); then there was Paget's Lane and Red Hill, only perhaps twenty minutes' walk away. First we had to cross the railway at a level crossing. This lent an additional thrill to the excursion, for though it was only a single line track and trains very infrequent, a dark tunnel lay not many hundred yards away from the crossing, inviting, yet sinister. Incidentally, the railway was one of the factors which contributed to the quietude and isolation of old Tewkesbury, for the station had been built a mile from the town, since our forefathers had held up their hands in horror at the thought of their peace being disturbed by a snorting, roaring steam engine. But the long drive from Uplands led straight to the railway, so that we became familiar with the slow passenger train which ponderously plied its way between Tewkesbury and Malvern.

Red Hill lay beyond, just over the main road; here high red sandstone cliffs rose sheer above the River Severn, and there was only a narrow pathway between cliffs and river, so that we had to walk in Indian file. It was an exciting experience, and the knowledge that here grew woad, the only locality in England where that rare plant was still to be found, made it all the more exciting. We knew that the Ancient Britons used the dye from this plant to colour their bodies blue (though the actual flower is yellow). Beyond Red Hill lay Paget's Lane, an overgrown green lane, running parallel with the little railway. I associate it in my memory with dog roses, which grew in profusion there; but I am sure that for John it was a treasure house for all manner of more unusual wild flowers, all of which he would have been able to name, probably in Latin as well as English. I remember that his botanical Bible was *John's Flowers of the Field*, profusely illustrated and very comprehensive.

Much of his early knowledge must have been gleaned from those closely-printed pages.

John had been a very delicate baby; indeed his early infancy must have been precarious in the extreme, as my mother was unable to feed him herself and he was therefore reared by what used to be termed a 'wet nurse'. Ada Brick, who had been cook to our great-aunt, performed this duty and obviously performed it well. He was weaned on goats' milk, which a kindly old lady who kept goats supplied daily from her home on the Mythe, close to Uplands. For the first ten years of his life John was regarded – probably entirely without foundation – as 'not at all strong'. Cheltenham, to which my mother took us to live following my father's death in 1918, did not suit him. 'Too relaxing', pronounced the doctor, and, with profound wisdom, my mother steeled her heart and sent him to one of the toughest preparatory schools in the West Midlands, the Elms at Colwall near Malvern, where there was an outdoor swimming pool used by the boys in all weathers, and an attitude to health which proved to be the making of the so-called delicate little boy.

He soon became transformed into an outwardly very tough young schoolboy; swimming, playing cricket and football, involved in all the outdoor pursuits, both legitimate and otherwise, which the Elms afforded. Nevertheless, he retained his sensitivity, his inward love of the written word, his sometimes solitary approach to the wonders of nature (during the holidays he would go off by himself for hours after dark, 'sugaring' for moths, and pursuing in daylight all aspects of natural history), and all the while his love for Tewkesbury and the surrounding countryside deepened.

His literary tastes were at that time fostered in no small measure by his English master, Mr Churton, of whom he wrote at length many years later in *Portrait of Elmbury* and *Brensham Village*. Subsequently, at Malvern College, he had the incalculable good fortune to be taught by that eccentric character, 'Bingo' Banks, who took a genuine interest in his writing and proved of enormous assistance. Whilst still at Malvern John was writing regularly, at the age of fourteen or fifteen, for the *Malvern Gazette*, chiefly short poems in which his perception and love of words were even then very apparent. I was myself at Malvern Girls' College, with an elocution mistress who was imaginative enough to allow us eleven year olds to choose works from any of the poets to recite in class. I chose one of John's poems and stood up proudly to declaim *'Ode to a Trout'*, by John C. Moore, a performance which was still recalled by that elocution teacher forty years on.

When my father died, at the comparatively early age of fifty-six, my mother had been obliged to sell our beloved home, Tudor House (at the now unbelievably low price of £1,100). The oak panelling and historic carved overmantel of our day nursery were ripped out by the purchaser and sold to America. And although John and I had been convinced that a secret passage lay behind a hollow-sounding panel beside the fireplace, no such passage was revealed. So much for childhood's fancies!

Inevitably, when John departed for his preparatory school our ways diverged, and when he returned for the school holidays he had his three hard-bitten little friends, Dick, Donald and Ted, with whom to pursue his occupations. I, too, had found my own friends, one of whom owned a pony which was a great additional attraction, so that at this period our paths crossed infrequently. I was occasionally allowed to play cricket with the exalted male company, and sometimes accompanied John to the Tewkesbury cricket ground to watch the Gloucestershire team, of which Charlie Barnett, senior, was our hero.

Then came three years at Great Malvern, 'to educate the children', but it was three years of exile, and, as usual, we returned to our native Tewkesbury as soon as it was possible. My mother was almost as much a part of the Old Tewkesbury as the Abbey itself and was widely loved and respected in the town, where she was known as 'Mrs Cecil' to distinguish her from the numerous other 'Mrs Moores' living there in those days. An appreciation of her in the local newspaper quoted Chaucer's words: 'She used gladly to do wel. Such was her manner every day.' She was the most important influence of our young lives, for, a widow after only thirteen years of marriage, she had all the responsibility of bringing us up. She was left with considerably less money than had been foreseen and the sale of Tudor House must have been a great sorrow to her. She spoiled us unashamedly, and unashamedly we adored her for it. Her death in her 85th year in 1958 shook John deeply, for he was devoted to her and quoted her frequently in his books.

Finances would not permit John to remain at Malvern College beyond the age of sixteen, and it was planned that he should join the family firm of Moore and Sons (of which he was one of the 'Sons'), established as Estate Agents in High Street, Tewkesbury during the 1700s. But John would have none of it. He wished to write and write he would. After about three years he announced that he was going to set himself up as a freelance journalist, and despite almost overwhelming opposition, he gained his objective. No doubt the knowledge acquired during the reluctant spell at Moore and Sons (particularly, perhaps, a deep understanding of human nature) stood him in good stead in subsequent years, when he began to write in earnest. In an appreciation of him written by the well-known author, Richard Church, it was said: 'His marvellously detailed knowledge of rural affairs and his close contact with the folk of the West Country is partly due to his experience as a member of his family estate agency.' I am sure that this was true.

He used to say that, at the start of his career as a writer, he could have papered his bedroom with editors' refusal slips; a discouraging enough beginning, but writing was in his blood and he persevered unrelentingly until, at the age of twenty-three, he published his first novel, *Dixon's Cubs*, with Messrs J. M. Dent. This was to be the forerunner of some forty books in all.

For a time he went to live in London, writing almost with desperation; essays, articles, reviews, anything that came to hand; but he was never happy for long away from the countryside and his much-loved Tewkesbury. The crusading spirit was strong within him, and, never slow to take up a 'cause', rightly or wrongly, he flung himself wholeheartedly into the Spanish Civil War of 1936 as a freelance journalist. Returning to Tewkesbury, and still writing (indeed, he published fifteen books before, in 1939, the Second World War interrupted his career), he learned to fly at Staverton, then a Flying School near Cheltenham, and joined the Civil Air Guard. For a long time before war was declared, he was convinced that it was inevitable; and the signing of the peace treaty of Munich was to him no miracle, as he claimed that 'sentimentalists were only too willing to call it', but a shameful and sickening betrayal.

Eric Linklater wrote of him: 'Nothing in humanity was alien to him; nothing but cynicism'; but I would also add that he detested anything bogus – 'phoney', I think he would have called it. That was one of his words, and one of his chief dislikes. And so, Munich was phoney, and before long we were plunged into what came to be known as the 'phoney war'; that phase of inactivity when nothing seemed to be happening and yet we were living uncomfortably with all the trappings of war – black-outs, rationing, evacuees. Two days before the outbreak of war he joined the Fleet Air Arm, in which service he was to become a pilot, and a Lieutenant-Commander in the RNVR. Considerably later, he served at the Admiralty and was on the invasion planning staff, besides being commissioned to write the official history of the Fleet Air Arm.*

It was while he was working at the Admiralty that he met a Wren, Lucile Douglas Stephens. She was Australian, and in 1944 they were married. She was the perfect wife for him, sharing his interests; both beautiful and talented and loving literature, drama and country life.

When the war was over they went to live at Kemerton, a lovely village nestling beneath Bredon Hill (the Bredon of Housman's *Summertime on Bredon*), only some five miles from Tewkesbury; first, at Upper Kemerton in a Georgian house, Kemerton Lodge, and then, in 1960, at the Lower Mill, surrounded by ducks and all manner of fowl on the picturesque little millstream. With his cats which were adored by both Lucile and himself, he lived an idyllic life, writing (above all, and he had disciplined himself to work in what were virtually 'office hours'), riding, shooting, fishing, cricketing, maintaining his love of, and knowledge of, natural history in all its aspects. By now he had achieved his goal and was acclaimed as a leading writer on the English countryside. In 1946 the book which really established him was published by Messrs W. H. Collins. This was *Portrait of Elmbury* (the thinly disguised Tewkesbury from his childhood days up to the war), to be followed swiftly by *Brensham Village* (this was a synthesis of villages around Bredon Hill), and *The Blue Field.* The trilogy became widely popular and went into many editions, both hardback and paperback; whilst the BBC bought the television rights and produced a play which was so well-received that a second showing was given a few months after it was first seen. This TV success came after John's death in 1967. It was sad that he did not live to see it. He was, after the war, closely involved with broadcasting for many years, writing plays for both radio and television, and broadcasting frequently.

He worked extremely hard. His novels were all-important (one, *September Moon*, sold 500,000 copies); but besides these he used to write weekly articles for the *Birmingham Evening Mail*, which were redolent of the English scene and which were continued until the week before his death. Hard work was a necessity to him now. He had a wife and a comparatively large house; Lucile had contracted a form of TB during the war which, though happily cured, meant that she required all the care which he could provide. Nevertheless, his boundless energy was

*In 1945 he took part himself in the D-Day landings, in 'Operation Mulberry'.

also being diverted into fresh channels. In one of his books he remarked that he believed it to be a virtue in itself to do as many things as possible. He had always possessed a deeply aesthetic side to his nature, and his love of the arts had led him to organize the Tewkesbury Play Festivals in the 1930s. In 1949 a new interest came into his life when he became Honorary Artistic Director of the first Cheltenham Festival of Literature, a position he held for many years. He was Chairman of the Festival Committee for a number of years after its establishment, and judged the modern poetry competition there. The annual Festival which still takes place is a lasting memorial to him.

Inevitably, this venture brought him into close contact with the leading writers of the day, and his life was enriched by an incalculable number of friends, not only from the world of literature, but from almost every conceivable sphere. These included Amy Johnson (that intrepid woman who was the first to fly solo to Australia); Cecil Day-Lewis and Stephen Spender who were friends from the Spanish Civil War; W. Bridges Adams, Director of the Stratford-on-Avon Festival for fifteen years; Arthur Bliss (Master of the King's Music); Eric Linklater; Compton Mackenzie; Richard Church; Laurie Lee (author of *Cider with Rosie*); the poet Louis MacNiece; Tim White (whose enchanting books were transformed into that popular musical, *Camelot*); Ludovic Kennedy and his ballet-dancer wife, Moira Shearer; Sir John Betjeman (who said in a broadcast about John that he could never remember the first time he met him; he seemed to have known him for ever), and that dear, kind ornithologist, one of the greatest of the century, James Fisher. Of him I shall always think with gratitude, for he was returning from an expedition to the Antarctic when he heard on the radio of John's death. As soon as he set foot in England he collected his car and instead of going home drove like Jehu in order to come with us to the funeral service in Tewkesbury Abbey. Of course there were many more besides these, for John had a great capacity for making friends, and, having made them, keeping them. But they were not, by any means, all 'famous men'. His friends were also numbered among the villagers, among the townspeople of Tewkesbury, even among the poaching fraternity. Eric Linklater wrote, in his book, *John Moore's England*, 'Tewkesbury was his home-town, the heart of his own country, and John knew everyone who was worth knowing, there or within a dozen miles of its soaring splendid Abbey. That became evident on Saturday night [during a weekend when Mr Linklater came to stay] when we were walking back from Bredon. We had spent a very happy evening in a crowded, friendly pub called the Fox and Hounds, and when we were on our way home a figure emerged from the darkness of a hedge and in a soft Gloucestershire accent a voice said '"Evening, Master John". John recognized either man or voice, and answered "Hallo, Dick. Had any luck?" A mile or two farther on, the same thing happened again, though this time it was "Hallo, Charley" and I realized that these dimly-visible, mysterious figures, materialising from the dense, unbroken darkness of hedge and ditch, were local poachers, all of whom knew John, as John knew them.' In today's world, the poacher is a very different kettle-of-fish: high-powered, sophisticated and ruthless; but John's poachers were humble folk, probably with large families to feed — before the years of the Welfare State — and were simply poaching a rabbit or two for the pot, and that nobody, least of all John, would grudge them. Indeed, they poached his own small shoot shamelessly!

One of John's characteristics was the typical long stride of the countryman. I can well remember him being reprimanded by my mother when he was a boy, for 'slummocking'. This is an old Gloucestershire dialect word and signifies something between a slouch and a shamble. My mother would, no doubt, have heard it as a girl in the rural community of North Gloucestershire in which she lived as a doctor's daughter in the last century. Curiously enough, the Mayor of Tewkesbury, who wrote a tribute to John in the local paper after his death, mentions this peculiarity. 'We shall miss his presence . . . most of all we shall miss meeting him in our streets, walking along with his own particular gait.'

He had never ridden regularly, but towards the end of his life he bought himself a little blood mare, Zena, whom he rode all over Bredon Hill and the surrounding vale. He derived immense pleasure from her and lived to see her first and only foal, whose birth he witnessed and subsequently wrote about as though it were something of a small miracle. All nature was a miracle to his receptive mind.

John was a passionate conservationist — many long years before this now rather over-worked word became universal and even somewhat abused. He was philosophical with regard to some aspects of the changing countryside; for example, when I deplored the erection of pylons which stretched across the Ham, he accepted them as the March of Progress, and therefore inevitable. He was nothing if not a realist and evolution cannot be halted. In one of his earlier books, *The Countryman's England*, published shortly before the outbreak of Hitler's war, he wrote these words: 'It's no use regretting the passing of Merrie England or trying to revive it. You can't be Merrie when you're dead.' He was, however, infinitely less tolerant of the indiscriminate use of lethal sprays, pesticides and insecticides on the land, and as long ago as the late 1940s he was prophesying that man was beginning to destroy the countryside and indeed the world. His voice joined with that of Rachel Carson, who wrote her prophetic *Silent Spring* in 1963, in condemning this threat to wildlife. Theirs were voices crying in the wilderness in those days, but how right they were it is left to a later generation to judge. His most appropriate memorial is that of Tewkesbury's lovely little Countryside Museum dedicated to his name and opened by his friend Ludovic Kennedy in 1980.*

It was in 1966 that perhaps his best novel – and, sadly, his last – was published. It had taken him three and a half years to write and was a notably long book of nearly quarter of a million words. John's publisher, the late Billy Collins of Messrs W. H. Collins, was due to go to Australia on a business trip and was anxious to read the script before leaving England; but when there were only some 10,000 words left to write John became ill and it seemed to be touch-and-go whether the book would ever, in fact, be printed. 'I lay in my bed', John recalled later, 'and thought about my overdraft and how very absurd it would be if I pegged out with the book so nearly done, not worth a penny until the last sentence was written, but worth perhaps quite a lot to my dependants thereafter. Anyhow, I recovered. The book was done. My English publisher read 220,000 words in three days and rang me up late at night to say he was going to print more copies than he had ever printed of anything of mine before.' Mr Collins' faith in *The Waters Under the Earth* was fully justified. A best-seller in America, it was also chosen in its German translation, as the Book of the Month by the most important book club of that country. It was printed in no less than seven languages.

Though professedly an agnostic, John applied Christian principles to his life in a remarkable way, and was always willing to give a helping hand to anyone in need. To the many strangers who wrote or called on him asking to have their copies of his books autographed, he always acquiesced with some appropriate comment or message. He once gave me a sermon on Love which far surpassed the majority of pulpit sermons; universal love was his theme (even extending to the unspeak-

*See page 22.

able boy who had just earned my undying hatred by shooting a nuthatch).

His overwhelming love of the English countryside which began in the 'Elmbury' of his early childhood, continued all through his life, and his final words in *Portrait of Elmbury* read: 'I am glad to have belonged to it, to have been part of it.'

BOOKS BY JOHN MOORE

Dixon's Cubs, 1930
Dear Lovers, 1931
Tramping through Wales, 1931
King Carnival, 1932
English Comedy, 1932
The Walls are Down, 1933
The Welsh Marches, 1933
Country Men, 1935
The New Forest, 1935
Overture, Beginners, 1936
The Cotswolds, 1937
Clouds of Glory, 1938
The Countryman's England, 1939
A Walk through Surrey, 1939
Life and Letters of Edward Thomas, 1939
Wit's End, 1942
Fleet Air Arm, 1943
Escort Carrier, 1944
Portrait of Elmbury, 1945
Brensham Village, 1946
The Blue Field, 1948
Dance and Skylark, 1951
Midsummer Meadow, 1953
Tiger, Tiger, 1953
The White Sparrow, 1954
The Season of the Year, 1954
The Boys' Country Book (edited & partly written), 1955
Come Rain, Come Shine, 1956

Jungle Girl, 1958
Man and Bird and Beast, 1959
The Year of the Pigeons, 1964
The Waters under the Earth, 1965
Among the Quiet Folk (published in USA, 1967
   Subsequently in UK), 1984
The Angler's Weekend Book (in collaboration with Eric Taverner)
The Book of the Fly Rod (in collaboration with Hugh Sheringham)

The John Moore Museum

Church Street Tewkesbury

A Countryside Museum

Open Tuesday - Saturday
10am-1pm and 2pm-5pm

PROLOGUE

The varied threads which went to make up the tapestry of John's boyhood and youth were as diverse and many-hued as those fishing flies in his fly-box, of which he wrote so often and so lovingly.

Since these threads obviously influenced his subsequent life to a considerable degree I have gathered them together, interwoven as they are in a colourful tapestry, and let them create, as it were, the background to this book.

'The Colonel', who walks through the pages of so many of John's books – or perhaps I should say more truly, *hobbles*! – was no apocryphal figure but a real, flesh-and-blood individual; and in spite of the disparity in their ages (I suppose that the Colonel was about forty years John's senior) their friendship became one of the most treasured things in both their lives. 'I learned from him', declared John in his *Portrait of Elmbury*, where we first meet this redoubtable character, 'more than I ever learned from any schoolmaster.' Together they shot, fished, 'pottered about' in the countryside, enjoyed the diverse company and warm fellowship of the Swan bar at Tewkesbury.

He really deserves a section to himself, but this would not be feasible, since he accompanies John in so many of his country pursuits that he puts in an appearance under almost all the existing headings. You will come across him unexpectedly here, there, and everywhere in this anthology.

Like John, I also loved him dearly. We used to meet out otter-hunting with the Wye Valley when they visited the Tewkesbury area twice a year, and always he would have his little joke with me. . . . 'Have you dusted the drawing room mantelpiece, Daphne?' for there was a somewhat insubstantial agreement with my mother, during my early days spent with hounds, that I performed a few small household duties before leaving home. The answer to the Colonel's question was always in the negative and this fragile rule, always broken, was never enforced in the days to come.

As they pottered about in the country, so they talked, and if we eavesdrop on a conversation not long before the Colonel's death in 1938, we can understand what a fascinating companion he could be. . . . .

'As we walked along the garden path he bent down (it hurt him to bend, for he'd stiffened up after a long day's walking) and picked up an acorn. "Look at it, so neat in its little egg-cup – how perfectly it fits – how *pretty* it is – ever since

I was a child I've enjoyed staring at an acorn at least once a year!" We talked about the special things which gave us this particular kind of wonder or delight. Chestnuts just out of their spiny shells; hedgesparrows' eggs, said I, transparent blue like the tempera colour of the sky in an Italian Primitive painting; an orange-tip butterfly, said he, sitting on an umbel in the April sun. What about a green hairstreak, said I, wings folded so that the vivid underside shows, on a hawthorn-bush in May? Birdsong, said the Colonel; not the famous singers only, but the black-cap and the sedge-warbler and the jenny wren and her small unassuming song as she pauses for a moment along the hedge-roots? Then we talked of smells. Wet earth after a drought; tomatoes; bruised bracken; the smell of geranium leaves on your hands when you've been taking cuttings; the smell of a weir; stables; the apple-picking smell; a squitch-fire on an autumn evening.

'And so we went on. I didn't know then that the Colonel was dying; maybe he didn't know himself, when he added to our catalogue beech leaves in the spring, and the silvery buds on the wayfaring tree, and a glimpse of foxes teaching their cubs to play, and the affectionate purring noise which a sitting hen makes when her eggs are hatching. Did he have an inkling that he wouldn't see another May? Perhaps, but all seasons were sweet to him. . . .' (*Come Rain, Come Shine.*)

The Colonel was a weather prophet of such skill that many a television forecaster might have learned from him, despite their expertise in such matters as 'highs' and 'lows' and 'cold fronts' and 'warm fronts' and all the other paraphernalia of esoteric phrases with which their vocabulary is endowed.

'The Colonel' (wrote John in his novel, *Brensham Village*) 'always felt the weather in his bones. Suddenly he said: "It's going to freeze". "What, in May? Can you smell it?" "I don't know if I smell it or simply feel it in my bones", he said, "but it's going to freeze smartish and I'm frightened for the plums." And, of course, he was right; and the May frost destroyed not only the plums, but almost everything upon which the market-gardeners depended for a living.'

'Everybody loved him,' as John observed in the same book. 'I often wondered why, though I loved him as much as anybody. At first sight he was just a peppery old man who drank too much whisky; a rather ugly old man with a purple pimply nose and a tobacco-stained walrus moustache. But of course he was much more than that: a kind of greatness clothed him, though I was never able to define it nor to decide wherein his greatness lay. He had, beneath his peppery manner, a beautiful courtesy; but so did many other old gentlemen of his generation. He had a huge sense of fun, and a twinkle in his blue eyes, and his laughter bubbled like a spring, was such laughter as the Greeks called Ionian because it reminded them of the mirth and music of the mountain streams. But other men, after all, possessed merry blue eyes and laughed gaily. I think perhaps the Colonel's greatness had something to do with the fact that he belonged more completely than anybody else to the fields, woods, rivers which were his home. He know the ways of each thing that ran, swam, crawled or flew not as a man who has learned them but as if by instinct . . . Compassion: perhaps that was the secret of his greatness. His compassion extended to all living things, even – though this may sound absurd – to the creatures he hunted. I do not mean that he pitied the fox with the sort of anthropomorphic pity which sentimentalists feel who imagine it suffers the same terror as they would suffer if they were pursued by dogs. He *knew* the fox; he was at once the hunter and the hunted, just as he was farmer and labourer, landlord and peasant because of his compassionate understanding of all.'

BACKGROUND TO CHILDHOOD (1913–1918)

The loveliest house in Elmbury, which was called Tudor House, looked out across a wide main street upon the filthiest slum I have ever set eyes on in England. Few people saw anything incongruous in this, for in those days Elmbury was a higgledy-piggledy place, of incomparable beauty and incomparable squalor, and its inhabitants had retained something of the spirit of the Elizabethans, who could enjoy *Hamlet* in the interval between an afternoon at the bear-pit and a visit to the brothel, when both bear-pit and brothel lay within a stone's throw of the theatre.

In Tudor House I spent most of my early childhood. That is literally true, for apart from brief formal 'walks' with Old Nanny we didn't go out much, and since I was erroneously supposed to be 'not very strong' I was always in the condition of having a cold, of having had a cold, or of being liable to catch a cold if I got wet. So Tudor House was my world; and with its winding staircases, its dark oak-panelled corridors, its numerous exciting junk-rooms and attics, and its curious and delightful back-garden, it provided a domain wide enough for any small boy.

The garden, especially, was a child's paradise. It was not too big, so that we knew every stick and stone of it; and since it was by no means a source of pride either to our parents or to the occasional odd-jobbing gardener, we could do whatever we liked in it without reproof. Moreover, it had an unique and thrilling smell, a sort of jungle-smell made up, I suppose, of damp rotting leaves, wet sandstone walls, a stagnant well, and dead cats in the nearby river: you would scarcely term it a fragrance, but we loved it, somehow we associated it with adventure and mysterious things.

No doubt the extraordinarily high walls were the cause of the garden being so damp. One of these was provided by a Drill Hall wherein the local Volunteers ineffectually paraded once a week; another, of tremendous size, unscalable even by cats, was a bastion against our next-door neighbours: it need have been no bigger if the Picts and the Scots had been encamped on the other side of it. The third wall, most unnecessarily, shut out the slow river, with its barges, its rowing-boats, and its immobile patient fishermen. A great oaken door, however, which creaked terrifyingly like that which gives entrance to the home of the omnipotent gods, opened on reluctant hinges to these delights.

The high walls, which seemed to cloister the garden rather than to imprison it, were in themselves extremely beautiful. One of them was made of Old Red Sandstone, and the other two of the pinkish-orange Georgian brick which becomes almost incandescent and glows with an inward light when the sun shines on it. The Drill Hall was covered with Viriginia Creeper, its leaves redder than robins' breasts in autumn. The wall-against-the-neighbours was hung with ivy, a dusty hiding-place for sparrows' nests, for small yellow moths, and for those big downy brown ones called Old Ladies. The river wall, of weathered sandstone, was a background to the most delightful herbaceous border imaginable, a small-scale jungle in which peonies, stocks, marigolds and red-hot pokers fought for life, and out of which triumphantly rose great hollyhocks and even more gigantic sunflowers, a few of which each season topped the wall and, having looked towards the Promised Land, bowed their heads towards it and contentedly died.

For the rest, the garden possessed one climbable tree, a laburnum, seasonally weeping golden rain; a bush of white lilac; a sort of shrubbery about five yards square, just big enought for one thrush's nest each spring; white jasmine on an outhouse wall; a small wicket-scarred lawn; a 'sand-pit' in which we children were supposed to play (but we had better games); and a disused well, with an old ramshackle wooden cover to it, which we believed to be the entrance to a monks' secret passage.

Above the garden towered the big house. Its 'backs' were as beautiful as its façade. You went up some wide, semi-circular stone steps on to a flagged courtyard around which stood the half-timbered building, whitewashed between its sepia oak beams. The back door was a tremendous piece of oak, studded with nails, with a knocker heavy enough to wake the dead; there were strange scars on the oak as if someone with an axe had tried to force his way in. Inside there was a sudden cool darkness of stone-floored corridors, sculleries, pantries and whatnot, and then the spice-scented kitchen with Old Cookie, if she were sober, busy over her pots and pans. Then you came to the hall, its panelled walls hung with brass ladles, a curious form of decoration (but pictures would have looked cold and lonely against the dark oak); then, off the hall, the drawing room, very long and light, with big windows and a pale oak parquet floor – the walls abounding in more brass ladles, in copper warming-pans, shelves of pewter tankards, cabinets of valuable china, a housemaid's nightmare; and then the dining room, as cosily dark as the drawing room was airily-bright, with the royal coat of arms (we never knew why) carved above the mantelpiece.

THE COLONEL

Once a year, on Boxing Day, scarlet was the colour of pageantry when the foxhounds met outside the Swan Hotel and afterwards the whole cavalcade titttuped past on its way to the first draw, dappled flop-eared hounds, shining horses, shining leather, shining top-hats. In the summer there was sometimes a meet of the otterhounds, but this was less of an entertainment because there were no horses and no pink coats; instead the participants wore a blue uniform with scarlet stockings which even to us seemed rather odd. I remember chiefly some ferocious looking women, thus garbed, carrying long poles with which, I imagined, they must surely beat the poor otter over the head. I remember also a man like an elderly gnome who wore a faded green Norfolk jacket and knee-breeches, with a deerstalker hat of astonishing shape to match. These clothes, and something indescribable in the air with which he wore them, marked him without doubt as a man of the forest and the field. He caught my imagination at once, as some sort of older edition of Robin Hood. His face was red and his nose was a brighter red; he had a badger-grizzled walrus moustache and little twinkling blue eyes. We were told he was 'the Colonel'; we never asked what colonel, and it was years before I discovered his name. Then, as you will read, I got to know him well; and I learned from him more than I have ever learned from any schoolmaster. But I never forgot my first sight of him, when I watched the meet through the window (as usual, I had a cold). He arrived on a motor-bicycle, which he was unable to control. Skidding to avoid the hounds, he fell off. He picked himself up, grunted angrily, promptly produced a silver flask out of his pocket, and examined it carefully to make sure that it was unbroken. Then he shook it, holding it up to his ear, to make certain that its contents were undiminished. Then, to make doubly sure, he put it to his lips and swigged the lot. As he wiped his moustache he happened to look towards our window; and seeing my face there he suddenly grinned. His ribston-pippin cheeks all wrinkles, he looked like a kelpie. I was enchanted and I grinned back, but it was too late; the hounds were moving off and the Colonel with them, hobbling along on bowed legs and with bent back, as crooked as a hobgoblin.

COUNTRY PREP SCHOOL (1919–1924)

Shortly after this I was sent to school, underwent certain metamorphoses, and was transformed from a pampered and coddled brat into an extremely tough little ruffian. This was largely due to the glorious prep school, a gracious Georgian house in its own grounds about ten miles from Elmbury, where I learned to tickle trout and to read Virgil; to swim a length under water and to enjoy English history; all about catapults, and a little about Attic Greek.

The poaching, the swimming, and the catapult-shooting I acquired partly by the light of nature and partly through the companionship of three other boys, Dick, Donald and Ted, who had the reputation of stopping at nothing short of murder. The Latin and Greek I learned from a man who loved the classics and knew how to teach them. One day, when I had been consistently slow at finding the verb in my Latin unseen, he sent me to the Headmaster with a note. The note was folded but conveniently unsealed. Naturally I wanted to find out what had been written about me and what was my probable fate. I hid in the lavatory and tried to read it. But the sentence was in Latin. For the first time in my life it seemed really important to construe a Latin sentence. My mind worked at three times its usual pace, I found the verb more quickly than I had ever found the verb before, and when I had the hang of the sentence I was encouraged to continue on my journey towards the Headmaster's study; for it said: 'Do not beat him with too many stripes'.

This wise scholar, Mr Chorlton, had a cottage at Elmbury where he spent the holidays. He was a link with home, and for this reason I never felt exiled. The school was such a civilised place that terms passed quickly; and in the holidays I never wanted to go to the seaside, but always returned to Elmbury, where Dick, Donald and Ted were near neighbours.

And now with my new-found freedom and my awakened intelligence I began to find out more about Elmbury than I had ever known before. I explored the rivers and the brooks, the field-paths and the woodlands; discovered one by one the villages and hamlets; made friends of poachers and foes of keepers; and enjoyed a kind of Richard Jefferies boyhood in which holidays coincided with seasons and each season had its special delights. Easter holidays were birds'-nesting holidays (curlews and redshanks on the Ham; plovers on the ploughed land; finches in the hedgerows; whitethroats in the nettles; magpies and hawks in the highwood on the hill!). Summer holidays, long and leisurely, were divided between fishing and butterfly-hunting, swimming and 'messing about in boats'. At Christmas we followed the hounds on foot, skated on the frozen floods, learned to shoot rabbits (and other game) with .22 rifles, went ferreting with farmers, fished for pike.

I never minded going back to school; because school, too, was fun. But always, even at school, Elmbury was the background, its rivers, meadows and lanes were unforgotten, and with Dick, Donald and Ted in the dormitory at night I would plan next holiday's expeditions. We must make another attempt to catch the big carp in Brensham Pond; after that we'd hunt the old willows for Puss Moth caterpillars and Red Underwings; and when it grew dark we'd light lanterns and 'sugar' the trees in the rides for moths. We must tar the bottom of our old boat and make it watertight; we must go cubhunting in September, and we must ask Keeper Smith if he'd let us beat when Squire started partridge-shooting; we must camp at the Hill Farm and help Farmer Jeffs with his harvest.

Elmbury and its green-and-brown countryside were always the stuff of our dreams. I was getting to know the place as Highlanders know their deer-forests: 'every stick and stone'. I was growing my roots.

Portrait of Elmbury

THE FIRST DAY OF THE HOLIDAYS

Unfortunately for us boys, the opening of the fishing season occurred in the middle of the summer term; we could not share the busy preparation, the sorting-out of tackle, the ground-baiting on the day before, the pink feathery sunrise-clouds reflected in the river, the first roach or bream caught at the very threshold of the dawn. But on the first day of the summer holidays we always made up for our loss. From early morning until after dark we fished; and even so there was never time to visit all the familiar places, to try all the likely holes.

We would start off before the dawn in the *Sunshine*, an old tub of a boat that had been a Norwegian ship's dinghy before our parents acquired it, and the first thing to do, when we'd baled out our craft, was to drift down very slowly to King John's Bridge and dangle a worm before the noses of the big perch that lived in the shadow of the arches. That beginning was almost always the most exciting part of the day, chiefly, I suppose because it *was* the beginning. We lay in the bottom of the boat, and raised our heads so that we could just peep over the gunwale while we sent our worm on the end of a handline questing among the stems of the lilies. It was a terribly breathless moment when the perch came out of the shadows into the sunlit water – their stripes made them look like the skeletons of fishes – and it was difficult to be still when the big mouth opened and shut and lo! the worm was gone and the line was cutting a sharp V along the surface.

I don't suppose we should find it so easy to catch perch nowadays. Even on our primitive handlines we always had two or three, and often they weighed more than a pound apiece.

When King John's Bridge would yield no more we generally rowed upstream to the lock, where we put our rods together and fished in the white tumbling weir, or off the wall of the lock itself, or from the ruins of the old mill. Here the water was green and very deep; Leviathan, we felt, might lurk here. It was always an adventure to climb down upon the paddles of the disused mill-wheel and, hanging there, to flick a bait into the dark swirly eddy in the very corner of the wall. You went down out of the bright hot sunlight into the sudden coolness, the spray from a spout of water tumbling through a breach in the hatch tickled your face, and there was a nice queer cold rotten river smell, the smell of silkweed and foam and wet rotting wood and goodness knows what else all mixed up together. But the paddles were frail and creaky, and one day I was suddenly aware of another sound – a new groaning and creaking that came from the direction of the axle. I tried to climb up, but the wheel had begun to move, and the harder I tried to get up it the faster it turned. Slowly at first, then more swiftly, and to the accompaniment of horrible groans, as if its very heart were being torn out, it swung round, perhaps for the first time in a score of years. The noise was like the opening of the great door of the abode of the gods:

Panditur interea domus omnipotentis Olympi,

and half-way through the hexameter the groaning ceased and as the wheel moved freely at last I fell off it into the hissing swirling green deeps below.

But it was the first day of the holidays, and there was no question of going home; I fished naked while my clothes dried in the sun!

When we were tired of the weir and the lock we went downstream again, illegally trolling for pike on the way, and if there was enough water in the Piddle we generally explored it, for it was a famous place for little bleak and dace, and we used these as live-bait for perch and jack. Then we drifted down the shore of the Ham, and tied up the *Sunshine* while we fished at the mouth of the Swilgate estuary for roach and bream. By this time we had had enough of wandering, and were content to sit and watch our floats while the sky grew pale and the wind dropped and the lamps were lit in the Hobnails windows. We chaffed old Joe across the river each time he caught an eel, and talked to Reuben White the water-bailiff who came down the bank to greet us with his friendly grin: 'You young hooligans back agyun from schoo-ul! And now you'll be pestering the life out of me till September.'

'Caught any poachers, Reuben?'

'There warn't none, till you came back!'

'Any samlets going, Reuben?'

'If I catches any of you hooligans with so much as the *fin* of a samlet, I'll –'

We laughed. 'Poor old Reuben!'

It was nice to meet all our friends again.

And when the stars came out, and we paddled quietly back up the still river, we would talk, quietly now, of our plans for tomorrow. Tomorrow we would go and look for withy-bobs and fish for chub with them. Tomorrow we would try honey paste for the big carp in the Osier Bed pool. Tomorrow we would see if it was true, as Reuben had told us, that there were tracks of an otter with cubs at the top of the Swilgate Brook. Tomorrow we would visit Miles Hopton and find out if he had a ferret for sale. Tomorrow we would start ground-baiting a roach-swim off the Bloody Meadow. . . .

We hugged ourselves with excitement. Tomorrow, tomorrow! On the first day of the holidays it always seemed as if tomorrow would last for ever.

FLOUNDERS

Nature in her evolutionary processes takes a few hundred thousand years to modify a muscle, a few more hundred thousand to relieve one of her creatures of the burden of an unnecessary tail. Goodness knows how long it took for the flounder's starboard eye to traverse the inch or so round to the other side of his nose, so that he can lie on the sand and stare up vacantly through the water with two goggle-eyes on the same side of his ridiculous face. Perhaps a quarter of a million years.

It seems almost as long since flounder-fishing was one of the serious affairs of our young lives; since we used to go down to the Ham in April and fish with lobworms off Sandy Point. We were not, as it happened, particularly fond of catching flounders, but there was this important point in the creatures' favour, that there was no close season connected with them, so that they provided a cloak of respectability for the most flagrant pieces of poaching. You may be sure that if a boy of twelve catches a chub or roach in April (even if it's only seven inches long) it's cracked on the head and it goes into that remembered pocket which always smelled faintly of Miss Stevens' bull's-eyes. Thus the Law is broken, for the Law says that no one shall angle for chub, roach, and such-like coarse fishes between March 15 and June 15 inclusive. Flounders served as the sheep's clothing which we little wolves put on when we went fishing in April and May. Not even the astutest water-bailiff could penetrate our deceit. Reuben would say:

'Hey, you there, young hooligan, what are you doing with that rod?'

'Just flounders – flounders and eels.'

'Well, mind you don't take anything else.'

'Course not!'

I seem to remember something about samlets . . . but the Law has odd eyes like the flounder, and one looks backwards. Anyhow, no water-bailiff actually caught us.

And the flounders were not merely an excuse; we got quite a lot of amusement out of catching them. They were surely the most obliging

High Street (*above*) and Church Street, Tewkesbury, at the
turn of the century.

Tudor House, Tewkesbury, John Moore's boyhood home and (*below*) on the right of the picture, Tudor House as it is today.

little fishes in the world. They came all the way from the distant estuary and the vast sea itself so that small boys might catch them on worms. And lest the small boys should have neglected their rods, and gone off hunting for butterflies, they practised no sharp, wary bite like roach, no furtive sucking at the bait like bream; they just swallowed the worm, hooked themselves, and waited to be pulled out. Then they crowned their martyrdom by living, in a bucket or a large jam jar, for twice or thrice as long as any other of the captives of small boys had ever lived before.

The Countryman's England

SPORTING ENCOUNTER WITH THE COLONEL

It was out hunting that I encountered again that roguish, gnomish, remarkable man whom I first saw through the Tudor House window when I was a child: 'the Colonel,' whom I had since discovered lived at Brensham, where he had a small farm. 'Encountered' is the right word; for Jerry had put me on a horse which was too fresh for me, and it was running away with me down a steep lane on Brensham Hill when I met the Colonel coming up on foot. I did the best I could to avoid him, but the horse was going too fast; the sharp toe of my hunting-boot caught him right in the midriff and he collapsed with a loud grunt on the ground.

As soon as I had stopped the obstreperous horse I rode back to apologise. The Colonel had picked himself up, and if you can imagine an infuriated gnome you will understand how truly formidable he looked. I approached him timidly and penitently, hat in hand. He was making a loud spluttering noise which was not recognisable as speech. His long walrus moustaches bristled; his little blue eyes were popping out of his head; his face was purple, bright purple as a Victorian plum, and yet it had also a sort of pallor of rage which was rather like the bloom on a plum.

'I'm most awfully sorry –' I began; but that was as far as I got. If I was timid, my horse was thoroughly scared. It took one look at the

Colonel, flexed its ears, and shied; then, seizing the bit between its teeth, it spun round in the lane and galloped back madly down the hill.

SOCIAL ENCOUNTER WITH THE COLONEL

A few days afterwards I met the Colonel again in the Swan bar.

It was just before noon. The bar was empty and I settled myself in a chair in the corner with a pint of beer and *The Times* which happened to be lying on one of the tables. A moment later the Colonel entered. He took off his battered deerstalker, hung it up on a peg behind the door, and advanced towards the bar. He caught sight of me, his bright blue eyes stared angrily, he took three purposeful steps in my direction.

'Sir,' he said. '*Are you aware that you are sitting in my seat?*'

I hastily apologised – he was really a very terrifying old gentleman – and moved to a neighbouring chair. He grunted, ordered a whisky, and sat down. I thought I would placate him, and show deference to his grizzled hairs. I folded up *The Times*.

'Would you care to read the paper, Sir?' I said.

He glared at me. His moustache twitched. He looked as if he were about to spring, as if he would leap over table, chairs, whisky and all to assault me.

'*It is for that purpose, Sir,*' he said in a dreadful voice, '*that I order it to be delivered here every morning.*'

I was utterly abashed. I passed him the paper with mumbled apologies and tried to hide myself behind my beer. He was indeed a terrible and a wonderful old man; and I couldn't help admiring his gesture in having the paper delivered to the pub, where after all he spent half his time. (The other half was spent in the pursuit of various animals, birds, and fishes, during which *The Times* would have been an encumbrance.)

I became aware that he was staring at me over the top of his paper. I felt very frightened indeed; but as he slowly lowered the paper I perceived that his extraordinary face was undergoing a metamorphosis. A thousand wrinkles appeared all over it, as if a catspaw of wind blew across the sea. His blue eyes disappeared between folds of red weather-beaten skin. His turkey-cock neck shook and quivered. I suddenly realised that he was laughing. Out of his open mouth came suddenly such clear and merry laughter as I have never heard before, such laughter as the Greeks called Ionian laughter which matched the mirth of the Ionian springs. It was rare and beautiful and unexpected laughter and I was entranced as I had been entranced by his mischievous grin, some fifteen years before through the nursery window.

'God damn it, my boy,' said the Colonel, 'what a bloody old fool I am. Let's have a drink!'

REGULARS AT THE SWAN

I shall have much more to say about this remarkable Colonel, but first I must describe his habitat, which was the Swan bar.

Every country town has a bar like the Swan, but you will not find such a place in any city or suburb or village. It belongs absolutely to the small market town. It isn't a 'local', in the sense that villages and city streets have their 'local'; it has a different atmosphere altogether. It isn't 'commercial' and travellers avoid it like the plague. It isn't a stopping-place for motorists. And it certainly isn't a smart cocktail-bar.

You could call it a kind of Town Club; but people belong to it who would never be elected to any respectable club, and many good club-men are made so unwelcome that they stay away. It is not class-conscious in any ordinary sense; and yet one has the feeling that the people who regularly go there do represent a class. I cannot put a label to the class; I can only tell you who were the regulars in the Swan about 1930.

There was the Colonel; and he was certainly the Chairman, for he was the only one who possessed, as it were by prescriptive right, his own chair. There were two of his especial cronies, a genial fat lawyer called Johnnie Johnson and a merry little 'gentleman-farmer' called Badger Brown. There was Mr Chorlton. There was Mr Brunswick the haberdasher, There was the Mayor. There was his most active political opponent, a cobbler called Anderson. There were two or three more Town Councillors; a tailor; a jobbing carpenter; a pensioned sergeant-major; a retired gardener. There was Mr Tempest, the bank manager; Mr Rendcombe, the editor of the *Elmbury Intelligencer and Weekly Record*; and Mr Benjamin, a bookie, a Jew, and a good fellow who was generally in trouble with the police. And there was an idle little ruffian called Sparrow who ran illicit errands for Mr Benjamin, poached, and was reputed to be a dog-stealer. He lived in a caravan surrounded by ramshackle kennels full of barking and whimpering mongrels, which he had the impertinence to call the Sparrow Dog Farm.

These fifteen or so constituted the usual company at the Swan in the evening. There were others who dwelt as it were on the fringe; and of course there were occasional visitors, though strangers were not as a rule very welcome.

Now I cannot for the life of me tell you what it was that these members of the inner circle had in common. It wasn't class in the usual meaning of the word; for there were gentry, tradesmen and working-men. It wasn't politics, for the Mayor was a Die-hard and the cobbler was a Red. It wasn't money or the lack of it; for the lawyer and Mr Benjamin were both rich men, whereas the cobbler, the sergeant-major and the gardener were comparatively poor. It wasn't respectability, for Mr Benjamin notoriously kept two mistresses and Mr Sparrow occasionally went to prison. And it wasn't disreputableness, for Mr Chorlton was a Justice of the Peace and the Mayor was a Churchwarden.

Yet the company was homogeneous: so much so that if you entered the bar as a stranger you felt as if you had barged by mistake into a private room which had been hired for an annual reunion of old schoolfellows. And the longer you remained there, the more of an alien you would feel. These men of Elmbury didn't *mean* to be unwelcoming; they were kindhearted and friendly people. But because they were knit into so close a fellowship – by what mysterious bond I have never really discovered – they simply could not help appearing to a stranger to be a kind of secret society into which he had intruded.

And yet there was nothing sinister about their strangely-assorted companionship. They didn't, as you might imagine, order the affairs of Elmbury from the Swan bar. No council confidences were shared there. No tradesmen's secret deals were done there. No scandal was spread. The conversation of the Swan regulars was singularly innocent and inoffensive; being concerned chiefly with the following subjects:

The weather; the backwardness or forwardness of the season; gardening; crops; the price of plums; sprouts, and other local products; the behaviour of familiar beasts and birds; the rise or fall of the river and the likelihood of flood or drought; fishing; guns, dogs, horses and hounds; local topography especially in relation to Short Cuts (a most fruitful source of argument); old times, and their superiority in all respects over today; and, once more, again and again and yet again, the weather, past, present and future, yesterday's hailstones, this morning's white frost, the probability of tomorrow's thaw.

Prologue

THE RIVER-GOD

The Colonel and I had quickly become friends, and whenever the floods were out we went duck-shooting together in the evenings. The old man was bent and badly crippled with arthritis; his joints were as knobbly as the roots of a tree. But this did not prevent him from standing waist-deep in icy water waiting for the evening flight. He was sixty-five and it was a wonder he had survived so long; for he spent much of his time in the water, otter-hunting in the summer, duck-shooting in the winter, and at all seasons pottering about on his wet and marshy farm. The rest of the time he spent in the Swan: 'water outside, me boy, and whisky inside'. I have seen him crawl along a ditch *ventre à terre,* stalking a flock of geese, when the ditch was half full of water so that at times he was nearly submerged. I began to look upon him as a kind of water-creature: a river-god. It was wonderful to see him coming up out of the flooded meadows on a moonlight night after duck-flighting, crunching his way through the cat-ice, amorphous in his huge waders and loose-fitting jacket, deerstalker hat pulled down over his eyes. Thus must the Old Man of the Sea look when he comes ashore.

Geese were the ruling passion of his life. He would suffer any hardship, endure the utmost privation, for the chance of a shot at the grey-lags, white-fronts, and pink-feet which came to our meadows in great flocks during the late winter. When he had located a flock he would sit down and seriously plan a campaign against it. 'You've got to put yourself in their place', he would say. 'You've got to *think like a goose.*' Then, because I was silent he would look up and see my smile; his face would crumble away into that marvellous grin, and he'd say: 'Well, perhaps I do, perhaps I do'.

If there was snow on the ground he would wear his sister's nightdress for camouflage, covering his hat with a white handkerchief. Out of the whiteness his red face glowed and burned like a sun rising through the mist on the river.

He was – even at sixty-five – the best shot I have ever seen, the best stalker, the best naturalist, and incomparably the best fisherman. Yet his fishing tackle was almost as primitive as a schoolboy's. His greenheart fly-rod, which must have been as old as himself, had a kink in the middle joint and two kinks in the top joint; it was nearly as crooked as an apple-bough, or its owner's legs. But in his hands it was a magic wand with which he would conjure up fishes when nobody else could catch anything. In the little brook which ran through his farm, a mere runnel overgrown with reeds, bushes, and willows, he discovered a few trout where lesser men would have found only bullheads, gudgeons and eels. He caught two or three every season in the mayfly time, using only the top joint of his rod and dabbling a fly between the branches. The biggest was two and a half pounds, and he got it out from between the roots of a great willow. I swear that no other man could have landed it in such circumstances.

The Colonel didn't mind what he fished for so long as it swam, what he hunted so long as it ran, nor what he shot so long as it could fly. There were eels in his brook as well as trout and it was his custom to fish for them on Sunday afternoons, an otherwise barren time when there was no hunting and no shooting and the pub was shut. His method of fishing was original (for the Colonel was nothing if not experimental in his approach to every kind of sport). He used no less than six cheap cane rods, which he distributed at intervals along the bank. His lines were baited with lobworms. To each rod-point he fixed a small bell, such as might hang round the neck of a cat. He sat down in the middle of the line of rods, smoked his pipe, and took an occasional swig out of his flask of whisky. Whenever the *tinkle-tinkle* of a bell called him from his pleasant occupation, he strolled leisurely to the appropriate rod and landed his eel. He said that the bells, besides being useful, made the sport more exciting. The tinkling sound, now coming from one rod, now from another, now from two or three at once, gave to the pastime a sense of urgency which eel-fishing generally lacked.

Having caught his basketful of eels, and eaten them for supper, the Colonel nailed up their skins on his barn door and when they were thoroughly cured he oiled them and cut them into narrow strips and used them for bootlaces. I still possess a pair; and they are stronger and more supple than any other laces I have ever seen.

'A RAT! A RAT! DEAD FOR A DUCAT, DEAD!'

The Colonel loathed and detested rats. For all other animals, birds, and fish he had the queer sort of paradoxical friendly feeling that men have for the creatures they persecute. But rats he abominated. He used to sit for hours with his .22 rifle, stern and purposeful, waiting for the chance of a snapshot at a rat in the dusk. He rigged up in the rat-runs the most ingenious little springs of bent willow twigs with nooses lightly pegged to the ground; and again he would sit for hours in the hope of actually seeing a rat run into one. This, on the rare occasions when it occurred, gave him the most exquisite delight: to see the rat flicked high by the straightening twig, wriggling and kicking and swinging in the wind, like a highwayman upon the gibbet.

In his very last days rats obsessed him; and he wrote to me a short time before he died a postcard in which occurred the phrase, twice underlined: *Rats are getting at my walnuts.* But whether these were real rate or creatures of his phantasy I do not know.

FISHING

Angling is somewhat like poetry, men are to be born so . . .
IZAAK WALTON

John was no fishing snob. I really believe that he enjoyed his coarse fishing in the home waters around Tewkesbury as much as he did trout fishing in the lovely Cotswold streams and an occasional exciting foray after salmon further afield.

He had always fished . . . When he was very young there were the boating picnics which he describes in his books, when we hoped for pike or roach, but usually caught the ubiquitous eels – and when we were small children accompanied by our mother, *she* was always the one who had the unpleasing task of extracting the hooks from these slimy monsters!

He writes lovingly and with considerable knowledge of all aspects of the Gentle Art, and in 1931 he collaborated with the late Hugh Sheringham, a notable name in the fishing world, to produce a luxurious volume, most beautifully illustrated, *The Book of the Fly-rod*. This is now very rare, and, tragically, John's only copy was practically destroyed in the disastrous flood which swept through the Mill House at Kemerton about a year after his death in 1967. He was also joint editor of the erudite and entertaining *Angler's Weekend Book,* with Eric Taverner, published by Seeley, Service, and said to be 'unique in Angling literature'.

John did not think very highly of his own poetry – he probably under-rated it – but occasionally he would publish a few verses in a contemporary magazine. *Ode to a Blank Day* was first seen in *The Salmon and Trout Magazine,* and subsequently used in *The Angler's Weekend Book.*

Sadly, he left a clause in his will, directing that all his poems should be destroyed after his death; and this wish was naturally complied with, however distressing at the time. Consequently, many a good verse has been irretrievably lost.

ODE TO A BLANK DAY

Fortune, unkind to anglers, oft has frowned
On me before.
Believe me, I have got as great a store
Of wretched memories as any man:

The day I stumbled and was nearly drowned;
The grim remorse
After my line caught in the old tin can
When I had hooked Leviathan; and, of course,
The day at Tal-y-llyn
When I fell in
And found how cold Welsh water was in May;
And all the dismal ranks
Of hopeless and uncomprising Blanks –
The time I hooked and lost a dozen trout;
The bitter minute
When I had played a fish in Tay
For half an hour before the hook came out.
But ah! these memories simply are not in it
With you, incomparable day!
In fact you take
The blooming cake;
You beat the band –
You, to whose black and monstrous morn succeeded
A blacker afternoon
With hailstorms and
Snow (to remind
Me, were reminder needed,
That even rich and bounteous June
Could be unkind).
And then, when I
Thought I espied
A rift in the dark legions of the sky,
And walked a mile towards the little bridge
Where the big fellows lie,
You sent a still more evil eventide,
So that not one pale olive, not one midge,
Came out to exercise its fragile wings
(Which goes to show that even gnats and things
Are sometimes wise,
Wiser by far
When frail humanity.
And insignificant Ephemerida
Begin to think that it is rather odd
When June plays tricks with snow.)

Fishing

And then I broke my rod . . .
And, just as I'd decided I would go
(Being cold and wet),
I realised that I had left my net
Two miles away beside
The little tarn where I had lost three trout
That very morning on my setting-out;
So I went back there, swearing like Old Harry
And wondering which way
I'd choose for suicide –
The only adequate one was hari-kari,
As far as I could see.

O bitter and incomparable day!
You that had all
The winds of heaven at your beck and call;
Perfect epitome
Of all despair,
All wretchedness, all gloom, all misery;
Listen: I am not going to swear,
For I have sworn enough;
My splendid rage is spent,
And now I have a wondrous calm content,
(Though it was rather tough,
I think, to break my rod, a good split-cane;
But that's forgiven)
And I am almost happy, for I know
That though there may be days as bad again
There never can be worse.
Call on malignant heaven
To send its April and its August snow,
Its chilly rain,
I do not give a curse.
Let the winds blow
My olives and my delicate iron-blues
Out of their little box,
And I shall merely laugh.
Let me slip down on dangerous rocks
Into the swirling river; let me lose
My most expensive gaff,

My bag, my net, my reel,
I simply shall not care
A tupp'ny damn. I shall not even swear;
I'll merely say quite calmly (as I feel
My limbs for broken bones):
'A nuisance in a way –.
But still, of course, it simply can't compare
With that Remembered Day.'
And in quite gentle tones
I'll murmur to myself: '*This afternoon
Is nothing to the twenty-first of June.*'

And when I'm old and growing short of breath,
I'll tell the young'uns all the dreary tale,
Mumbling in my beard,
Sipping my port while they quaff foaming ale:
'There is no sting to Death,'
I'll say: 'There's nothing any longer to be feared,
For I have known the worst.'
And then I'll tell about the twenty-first,
And they, and their sons, and their daughters' sons,
Fishing for trout of infinitesimal size
With infinitesimal duns,
Will meet that cruel wench Fortune with a sneer,
And say: '*I know the weather's awfully dirty,
I know the fish won't rise;
I know I slipped and fell in at the Weir;
I know that weak seam in my waders burst;
But how about the fabled twenty-first
Of June, in Nineteen Thirty?*'

The Angler's Weekend Book

The weir is almost the only one of my boyhood haunts that doesn't change with the years. The woods I birdnested in are mostly cut down, the little new houses have sprawled out over the fields, much of the river-bank has been stripped of its willows by the destructive bulldozers of the River Board. But Elmbury Weir on the River Severn still looks the same, smells the same, makes the small dull thunder which if you listen to it long enough becomes a kind of noisy silence.

In March the elvers like short lengths of bootlace wriggle up the slack water at the edge of the current, and the elver-fishers go out by moonlight with their scoop-like nets of cheese-cloth to gather a profitable harvest of these tiny eels. There are salmon too, silver as new-minted coins, though for some reason they are uncatchable on rod and line. They swim on up the Severn and give sport to the anglers in the upper reaches; but at Elmbury they are only taken once in a blue moon more or less by accident by men fishing for pike or by small boys who are the darlings of the gods.

This is all the more strange since the Wye, which shares the Severn's estuary, and runs almost parallel with it on the other side of the Malvern Hills, is one of the best salmon-rivers in the world. In 1923 a young girl, Miss Doreen Davy, caught there a monster of 59½ lbs.; that's nearly the record salmon for England: a 60-pounder just beats it. But the record for Scotland is no less than 67 lbs., and this is how it stands in the fishing books that concern themselves with such things:

'*Salmon.* 67 lbs., caught in the River Nith, 1812, by Jock Wallace, a poacher.'

So Mr Wallace's fame has lasted for nearly 150 years, but because of his achievement, or his monumental piece of luck, his addiction to poaching is likewise remembered till Kingdom come. I wonder how the record became known. A poacher wouldn't normally advertise the fact that he had caught a whopper; but this salmon, I suppose, was *such* a whopper that he simply couldn't resist taking it down the pub, and weighing it on the pub-scales, and celebrating it with a dram or two, and taking the consequences, whatever they might be.

I've never understood Iago's riddling lines spoken to Desdemona:

>   She that in wisdom never was so frail
>   To change the cod's head for the salmon's tail;

unless cod, being sea-fish and therefore for most of the inhabitants of England scarce and expensive, was regarded as the greater delicacy.

Shakespeare certainly knew about the salmon of the Wye; for Fluellen says 'There is a river in Macedon; and there is moreover a river at Monmouth . . . and there is salmons in both'.

These famous salmon were also the subject of a remarkable legal action which the Law books call Chesterfield versus Harris and which, in the year 1906, fluttered the wigs of the learned judges in the Chancery Division, and of the Lord Justices of Appeal, and even the very important wig of the Lord Chancellor of England. It happened that for longer than anybody could remember the freeholders of a little Wyeside village called Hoarwithy had been accustomed to take salmon out of an eight-mile stretch of the Wye. They believed that the King had granted them this right; but they couldn't remember which King, nor when. It was certainly true they'd fished free for generations, and nobody had interfered with them. There were certain curious conditions attaching to the fishing: 'If they shall have taken any salmons they ought themselves to bring the same salmons to the Fish Board at Hoarwithy and remain there by the space of two hours before they bring the same salmons to any market or fair'. The Fish Board was a slab outside the village inn; and any pregnant women in the village had the right to cut a piece out of any salmon displayed there without payment! However, the old custom fell into disuse, and the fishermen got into the habit of taking their catches direct to the fishmongers at Hereford. This gave the Wye landlords their chance; the Earl of Chesterfield and others brought an action to restrain the Free Fishers. The case lasted seven days in the Chancery Court and the judge found in favour of the fishermen; but the Court of Appeal reversed the judgement, and so the persistent villagers of Hoarwithy carried their case to the House of Lords. Men who had never left their native village travelled adventurously to London-town and boldly stood up for their rights before the wigged Counsel and the grave judges. Their good broad Hereford accents must have brought a breath of fresh air into the stuffy Lords! At home, everybody in the village followed the case as eagerly as people follow the fortunes of their local football team. How sad it is to record that Hoarwithy lost!

'Your Lordships,' said Counsel for the landlords, 'are asked to assume a grant which did not exist, to a corporation which never existed, in order to assume a right which is unknown in English law. . . .'

All of which was doubtless true. There is something splendid all the same about this David-and-Goliath affair, and I don't much like to think of the homecoming of the village stalwarts, crestfallen that night in the village pub, telling a bewildered tale of how the men who 'fight by shuffling papers' had beaten them in a battle of which they didn't even know the rules!

Although the salmon are so disobliging at Elmbury, its weir is a kind of lucky dip from which, when schoolboys chuck out their random lines, they are liable to conjure all kinds of unexpected fishes. In May the twaite migrate up the river from the sea. They are very pretty fish, silvery-green, and weighing up to a couple of pounds. They will take a fly, but the boys catch them on a white feather or a hank of red wool attached to a bare hook. There are also flounders to be caught on worms. They are not often big enough to eat (though as a child I once took a monster which I sold to the fishmonger for sixpence, a sum for which in those days I could buy six hooks with gut attached!) Mostly they are of the size that can be accommodated in jamjars; and there our captives unhappily spent the brief remainder of their lives, lying on their sides at the bottom of the jar and looking up at us with a pair of reproachful eyes set, most oddly, both at the same side of the head.

Doubtless we perceived, young as we were, that this provision of two eyes on one side was not simply a whim of the Almighty but was the only sensible arrangement for a creature which spends nine-tenths of its time lying sideways upon the mud. In fact, however, the flounder isn't born like this. When it hatches from its egg it is the same shape as any ordinary fish – say a baby cod. As it grows up its cranium gradually rotates, carrying the orbit of the eye with it, until at last the left eye joins the other one on the right hand side of the head. This must be an odd experience; but it is an inescapable one if you are born a flounder and when it is completed you are well equipped to see what is going on as you lie upon the river-bottom, mud-coloured dark-side-up to camouflage you from your foes.

The flavour of the flounder has been likened to that of boiled wadding; and its chief claim to fame is that its female lays very nearly a million eggs (970,000, according to some expert who invented a way of counting them). This is more than any other flat-fish lays; and no doubt accounts for the fact that Elmbury Weir provides an unlimited number of flounders for small boys to catch. Grown-up anglers naturally despise them; and water-bailiffs heartily wish there were no such fishes for since they belong properly to the sea they are not coarse-fish within the meaning of the Act and so may be taken in the close season. This gives the small boys (and a few unprincipled elders) a good excuse when the water-bailiff comes along and reproves them for fishing at the wrong time of the year. 'Only catching flounders, Mister! – flounders and eel-uls!' But if I know small boys, they are fishing for whatever they can catch.

The strangest of all the inhabitants of the Weir is surely the lamprey, a mottled, hideous-looking creature about three feet long, with a sucking disc in its mouth, with which it attaches itself to other fishes, to stones, even to passing boats or to the sill of the Weir itself. You cannot catch it, of course, by ordinary fishing, but you can sometimes hook it out with a gaff, and a good cook will make a very tasty dish of it, though I believe this depends on a special recipe which only a few old Elmbury families still possess.

It was upon *lamperns,* I imagine, and not lampreys, that Henry the First surfeited himself till he died. These are much smaller, but are regarded as a greater delicacy. Incidentally, the city of Gloucester has an ancient obligation to send 'a dish of lamperns to the King on his succession and annually at Christmas'. King John fined the aldermen of the city 40 marks because 'they did not pay him sufficient respect in the matter of his lamperns'. The more dutiful Corporation during Queen Victoria's reign sent her a pie weighing 20 lbs 'filled with Severn lampreys, decorated with truffles in aspic jelly and crayfish upon gold spears.'

The sturgeon is another Royal perquisite which has been caught in the past in Elmbury Weir, though not for many years now. I was once told by some excited children that there were 'four or five enormous sturgings playing merry blazes in our bathing-place' and I hurried across there only to find a school of porpoises which had swum up from the sea.

It was delightful to watch them playing; and when I swam out to them they accepted me as another porpoise and played with me, barging me in a friendly way and splashing within a few feet of my face. I believe they are perfectly harmless, though they might knock the wind out of you if they became very boisterous.

After a few days in the Weir they vanished as suddenly as they had come; but ever since then I have felt that it is a place where almost any water-monster might appear, a Scotch kelpie or a Welsh afanc or Leviathan himself; even a Mermaid from the South Seas. But if *she* comes, sure enough some oaf will say to himself, as usual: 'Here's something strange; let's kill it' – and run home to fetch his gun.

Come Rain, Come Shine

SHIP'S YARD

Sam had a most ingenious method of ground-baiting his favourite holes up the river. He begs from the butcher a fly-blown sheep's head, ties it to the end of a long pole, and fixes the pole in an overhanging willow-tree so that it projects over the water. In the course of time the maggots hatch from their flies' eggs and whenever the wind blows the sheep's head swings to and fro and a little shower of maggots falls into the river. The fish are thus attracted to the spot, and three or four days later Sam visits it at dawn or sunset and reaps his harvest of roach and chub.

There is a sad story about Mr Shorrocks, the schoolmaster. It is said that one fine summer evening he rowed up the river with a lady, whom he was courting. (This happened a long time ago; Mr Shorrocks has given up that sort of thing, and now confines himself to fishing.) The lady was a schoolmistress from a neighbouring parish; it was very 'suitable' indeed, and at last the hour had come, the exact, the heaven-ordained hour, when he should propose to her. Having found the ideal and heaven-ordained place in which to do the deed, – a secret backwater screened by overhanging willows – Mr Shorrocks shipped oars, the boat slid silently beneath the boughs, and there in the green shade Mr Shorrocks cleared his throat nervously, remarked on the settled sky, the warm air, and the beauty of the overhanging willow trees, and prepared to unburden his soul. At last the moment arrived; it must be now or never; and with wildly beating heart and dry feeling in his throat Mr Shorrocks began:

'There's something, Edith, which I have been wanting to say –'

'Yes?' said Edith abstractedly.

'About the future, – er – *our* future –'

'Tell me,' she said. 'Have you noticed a very funny, a very *nasty* smell?'

'Listen,' said Mr Shorrocks wildly, 'Edith dear, I was just going to say –'

'*Something white and squashy and creepy-crawly,*' she said, '*has just fallen on my neck.*'

She seized the oars and paddled the boat out into the river; and Mr Shorrocks knew that the heaven-ordained moment had passed and would never come again. Very sadly and silently he paddled back in the gathering dusk towards the landing-stage above the bridge; and clickety-clack, clickety-clack, in the evening zephyr swung Sam's sheep's head.

SIGNS AND WONDERS

Mr Shorrocks is as unlucky in his fishing as he was in his love affair. He is one of those anglers, cursed of the elements, whom all the winds of heaven pursue, upon whom all rains deluge, and to whom all centres of depression gravitate. If ever you see Mr Shorrocks going fishing, you will be wise to stay at home; there is sure to be a cloudburst or a flood or an east wind.

But he is hounded by a curse far worse than that of the weathers. One might call it a curse of improbable happenings. He has been singled out by destiny to be the object of all the queerest and most ridiculous manifestations of chance. Signs and wonders follow his path as rooks follow a plough.

If there is in the whole of the neighbourhood at any given time one bat or bird so foolish as to mistake an angler's fly for the real thing, you may be certain that it will attach itself to the fly cast by Mr Shorrocks. If any strange sea-fish has wandered far inland up the river, it will seek out Mr Shorrocks' bait. If the river contains one object, animate or inanimate, that is the least bit out of the ordinary, Mr Shorrocks' pike-spinner will seek it out. He has, in his time, conjured from the very deep in this fashion half a tricycle, the remains of a typewriter, a boot, a cat, long dead, and a cardboard box marked 'Perishable, Please Keep Dry'.

And that is nothing. He alone of men was privileged once to look upon a very solemn and ritualistic evening rise of *eels,* two of which he hooked on a wet-fly. He captured a bream on a pike-triangle, hooking it through the back-fin. He shot the weir by accident and remained in his boat, seated and unconcerned, still casting his fly upon the turbulent waters.

He deliberately tempts the Fates. I was fishing with him one day, and he was finding life dull, I suppose, because nothing extraordinary was happening. There was a dipper sitting on a stone in mid-stream, about fifteen yards from him; and suddenly he looked at me and grinned. 'Can I? Can't I?' He swished his line through the air. One, two, three. 'Got him.' And there was the poor little bird dancing on the end of the cast. Yet in normal circumstances Mr Shorrocks could not cast accurately to save his life.

Last autumn he caught a corpse on float tackle. He was awfully pleased. He went about telling everybody how careful he had to be, landing it on 4X gut. There was an inquest, and a verdict of 'Found Drowned'.

Bats and dippers and water-voles are all very well; but I think that if I were Mr Shorrocks I should have given up fishing after the corpse episode. I should have felt that the Gods were playing a game with me, and that the Olympian sense of humour wasn't the same as mine. If I were Mr Shorrocks I should walk very delicately, lest Jove in jesting mood should suddenly heave a thunderbolt out of the sky.

THE LOCK

Like all unsuccessful fishermen, Mr Shorrocks always thinks that the farther he goes away from his home the more likely he is to catch fish. Familiar waters, he reasons, are empty and barren; has he not proved it by failing to catch anything for the whole of last week? But right up the river, farther than he has ever been before, there surely is El Dorado, there is the water bright with the silver and gold of flashing scales, there is the happy hunting ground where he will make the bag of his lifetime.

His reasoning, alas, contains several fallacies. The fact that he has caught no fish near the village does not, unfortunately, prove that there are none there; and in any case, if he fails in waters which he knows he is unlikely to succeed in waters which he doesn't know. But Mr Shorrocks doesn't see it that way; and so each season, led on like some old explorer by the desire to conquer the distant horizon, Mr Shorrocks goes a little farther up the river in vain search of his El Dorado.

The Countryman's England

THE CHUB

In winter you get chub by float-fishing. He is an omnivorous fellow. Silkweed, elvers, withy-bobs, bluebottles, grasshoppers, maggots, worms; cherries, cheese, live minnows; and an abomination consisting of pith from the backbone of an ox: he'll take whatever you offer him, and jolly glad to get it – if it's offered in the right way. But he's shy withal, so do not fish for him in cricket flannels. Also (in contradiction of popular superstition), he hates having thick gut heaved at him, with enormous flies on the end which throw up spray like a bursting shell when they hit the water. When this takes place within half an inch of his tail it is no wonder that he makes a great splash and disappears; whereupon the thrower of the fly exclaims: 'By Jove! . . . He nearly had it that time! He rose at it!' and continues to flog. People forget that chub possess nerves, like the rest of us.

The Angler's Weekend Book

The river was noisy, singing many songs; in between fishing they walked along it and watched the dippers. They were drab birds with very clean white shirt-fronts; they made Marianne think of shabby Soho waiters seen in the street in the morning. They found flowers, and Tim knew the names of all of them, old sweet names like melilot and plowman's spikenard. As they went hand-in-hand up the river Marianne thought that for her birthday she wanted nothing but this; but the gods had a gift for her in store.

She was sitting on the bank looking over the Willow-tree Pool. They had come back there towards evening. Tim was saying:

'The river's up three inches since this afternoon. You can tell by that rock in the middle.' It was loud too, its song now was a savage and mountainy one of Wales whence it sprang. 'Damn,' said Tim. 'I wanted that salmon for Father. It's what he likes best; and he's so sick now, he hardly eats anything at all.'

'Oh! Look!'

Just in front of the smooth rock the salmon leaped. It hurled itself into the air straight as a javelin, argent in the sun. Tim was down the bank before the boil in mid-river had died away.

'Quick!' he cried. 'You try for it.'

'No . . . You.'

'Come on. It's *your* birthday.'

She took his rod and waded out as far as she could. She felt the angry river tugging at her legs. She cast towards the smooth rock.

'Upstream a little,' said Tim.

Then the fish showed itself again. It was a big one, at least twenty pounds. Marianne's hands were trembling so much that she could hardly hold the rod. She cast upstream of the rock, twice, three times, four times: nothing happened. The fifth time she felt a little pluck. The spinner had swung round almost on to the rock, and she thought it had hit the rock, and she gave a tug to clear it. Just as she raised the point the rod jumped in her hand just as a water-diviner's twig is supposed to do, and the butt hit her hard in the pit of her stomach. Tim was shouting, and the rod was bent like a swan's neck, and her finger was smarting where the runaway line had ripped across it. The reel gave a loud protesting screech. Then Marianne saw the fish, going upstream like a torpedo, its back out of the water. She kept the line tight but the salmon cruised at will round the top of the pool; after a minute or two it came back towards her so that she had to reel in fast, and then in a sudden access of panic, the first alarm it had shown, it shook its head, tore away from her, leapt twice ('Dip your rod-top!' shouted Tim) and then plummeted down, down, down into the depths of the pool. It felt so heavy on the arched rod that Marianne was sure she would never get it up again; it must be right on the bottom now, sulking and lying still. She put on as much pressure as she dared, and although there were sixty yards of line between her and the fish she could still feel it shaking its head. That was a rather eerie feeling. Tim came out into the river and stood beside her. Just then the salmon set off once more, downstream now and very fast, so that the line made a little hissing sound as it swished through the water, cutting a V there and throwing up a tiny spray. The reel began to scream again as the line ran out. The fish felt heavier than ever with the current to speed it along. Tim said:

'Can you manage? You'll have to run.'

She nodded and set off downstream after the salmon. Tommy's waders were steadily filling with water, and as the buoyancy left them they felt as heavy as lead. She stumbled twice on the rocks, and once she thought she had lost the fish as the line went slack suddenly. Then it became taut again, and Marianne was off in pursuit of the fish, twenty yards of splash and scramble, right down to the bottom of the pool. There was shallow water here, and a lot of jagged rocks were showing; if the fish went between them the rocks might cut the line. So Marianne leaned back and raised the rod-top and hung on. There was an awful moment when she thought something must surely break; she was pitted against the salmon, it was now or never, the rod-top dipped, dipped towards the river. And still she held on. Then the strain gradually became less and she knew she had won. Tim had run down the bank to her, he had the gaff in his hand, and he was pointing to the slack water at the edge of the shallows. She looked where he pointed and there was the salmon's back fin, like a little boat's sail, moving very slowly in a semi-circle towards the bank. Marianne reeled in, and the brown sail came tacking across the current until it was directly downstream of her, and not five yards from the rod. Tim went down the bank and stood above the fish. It plunged when it saw him and that last plunge took Marianne unawares – the point of the rod went down until it was nearly touching the water. But the long tug-of-war in the turbulence at the tail of the pool had tired out the salmon; now it began to come up out of the deeps it had been desperately seeking, inch by inch, foot by foot, as Marianne fought it. She remembered riding Tim's horse and heaving its head up when it ran away – this was just the same feeling. As it came to the surface the fish turned over on its side, lashing feebly with its tail; Tim with the gaff at arm's length struck like a heron, then he was struggling up the bank with the fish dangling from the gaff and Marianne was squelching after him reeling in the line as she ran. Tim carried the salmon well into the meadow for safety's sake before he laid it down. Marianne's heart was thumping, her legs ached, she felt the water in the waders cold about her knees. She threw herself down in the grass beside the salmon. It lay there gasping, deep-sided, enormous, bright as a new-minted coin. She slid her hands beneath it and lifted it up to feel its weight; it gave a kick in her hands and she thought again of the slippery baby kicking. It was queer how that memory still delighted her. But the salmon was three times as heavy as the baby.

Even as Marianne balanced it in her hands, trying to guess the weight of it, the hooks came out of its mouth and the artificial minnow fell to the ground.

'Who's lucky?' Tim picked up the minnow and dangled it in front of her, so that she could see how one of the hooks had straightened, pulled out perhaps during the salmon's last plunge; like that, it could have had only the flimsiest hold. 'Just one more wriggle,' said Tim, 'and you'd have lost him.'

'It's my birthday! Nothing can go wrong today,' she said, and on their hands and knees, with the salmon on the grass between them, they looked into each other's eyes and laughed. Then Tim got up and pulled off her waders as she lay on her back and kicked her legs in the air. 'Skin a rabbit!' Pints of water poured out of them. Tim said :

'I'll take you home to change in ten minutes. I've got something I want to show you first.'

September Moon

When the rime is on the rushes, and the cat-ice makes a crinkly margin to our slow-running rivers, I am amazed afresh by the intrepid behaviour of him whom I know by no other name than The Frozen Fisherman.

His is the strangest of hobbies, for I doubt whether anybody, even the masochistic Mytton, ever inflicted such tortures upon himself in the name of sport. Each Sunday during the winter he bicycles out from his dark industrial city, and arrives in the village, frozen stiff, round about dawn. He collects the enormous bucket of live bait – roach, bleak and gudgeon – which the local Jack-of-all-trades has caught for him, and lugs it down to the river nearly a mile away. Here he embarks in a leaky and precarious punt, a vessel as austere as doubtless Charon's is, having the minimum of freeboard and being smeared all over with tacky black tar. It is also very unhandy and takes half the morning to extract from the muddy backwater in which it is moored.

Anchored at last in the wind-whipped middle of the river, the tenacious fisherman rigs up his complicated tackle, which includes a rod nearly as thick as a hedge-stake and a cork float the size of a turnip. With hands as red and raw as beefsteaks he dabbles in the bucket, seizes one of the cold slimy captives, and impales it upon his hooks. (But who shall say which feels the greater discomfort, he or his victim?) Then he proceeds to cast from a reel which often jams, causing the bait to fly off the hooks and the hooks to catch him between the shoulder-blades or in the nose or in the bowler hat, that unsuitable headdress which nevertheless seems to express his curious personality. At other times the reel runs too freely and the line snarls itself into a bird's-nest tangle which takes his numbed fingers half an hour to unravel. But with infinite patience he achieves his purpose in the end, and by then it is time to bale out the sinking punt. He bales for twenty minutes and picks up his rod again only to discover that the bait is dead or caught in the weeds. He reels in, impales another, casts out, and resumes his baling.

It is very rarely that he gets a bite, but when he does the event is spectacular, for the pike is a violent and precipitate fish – 'Mosstrooper-like he murders all he meets with,' wrote Richard Franck in 1694. The big float goes down with a resounding *plop*, and the fish is hauled in without ceremony upon the unaesthetic rod that not even a tarpon could break or bend. The 'play' which trout-fishers delight in means nothing to the bowler-hatted man; it's the bite that matters, and above all the *plop* of the disappearing float which he describes enthusiastically as 'like the cork coming out of a champagne-bottle'. This, clearly, is his moment of apotheosis. For this he endures the wind and the rain, the chapped hands, the grisly business of impaling the little fishes, the waterlogged punt and his perpetual snivelling cold; and on the infrequent occasions when it happens he becomes exalted, and a strange light shines in his bleary eyes. I have seen this shining look transform him when he was recounting the circumstances of the bite to our villagers in the pub. He came in, shivering and soaking wet as usual, and dumped his unlovely fish on the counter; for oddly enough he has no further interest in the pike when he has caught them, and believing them to be unwholesome he gives them to the landlord to feed to his hens. 'The float,' he said, as he sipped his half-pint of beer, 'lay as idle as – what does it say in that pome? – "a painted ship upon a painted ocean"; and suddenly hey presto, *plop!*' The light came into his eyes then, and he added as we knew he would, 'Just like a cork coming out of a bottle of champine'. It's an unexpected simile, because he doesn't look as if he had much experience of champagne. Perhaps he remembers some sister's or brother's wedding when the corks popped gaily; perhaps they popped at his own. Or perhaps he has never tasted champagne in his life, and the phrase is just Poetical – for did not Izaak Walton say that angling is like poetry, men are to be born so? And indeed, the little bowler-hatted fisherman who quoted the Ancient Mariner had one more remembered tag of verse with which he astonished us in the pub the other day. Goodness knows where it came from, that pompous fragment of eighteenth-century poetasting, which sounded so strange in the Horse and Harrow; but the little man fairly rolled it round his tongue. He had caught a particularly big fish, and when he had laid it on the counter he stood for a while admiring it.

'*The Pike, fell Tyrant of the Liquid Plain,*' he said suddenly: and then, as if conscious that he had committed a solecism, he gulped down his beer, put on his bowler hat, and hastened away.

The Season of the Year

FISHERMEN'S FLOWERS

It is only when the trout are rising very freely indeed that the primrose by the river's brim is a yellow primrose to us and nothing more. On such occasions, if we catch our fly in it, it may even be a blinking primrose; but we are not always so soulless, and when the rise is over we shall no doubt take an intelligent interest in it, and discover that it is not a primrose at all, but a yellow mimulus – for nobody but Mr Wordsworth ever saw a primrose growing by the river's brim.

But flowers have an importance to us fishermen which has nothing to do with botany. They are standard-bearers at the triumphal progress of our beloved river; they are banners at the march of our seasons; they are milestones in memory, so that we can tell, years afterwards, how we rose that two-pounder by the yellow water-lily in the bay. We mark seasons, times, places by them. The first cast at the trout is generally associated with the bright clumps of marsh marigolds which the country folk call kingcups or waterblobs, and which scorn to whisper of the spring, as the snowdrops and the anemones do, but seem to proclaim it with a mighty shout, like captives hailing their deliverer. There will be celandines at the time of the first cast also, on the bank underneath the hedge, and you will notice them when you pull on your waders and put together your rod. A few weeks later comes the time of the cuckoo and the cuckoo-flower. Our water-meadows go lilac then; and there is the whole spirit of April in those little flowers which some call lady's smocks and some call milkmaids. If I were banished to a far country, I believe I should remember England by her cuckoo-flowers, green meadows patched with lilac and the slow green coming on the willows, and a cuckoo calling very far away. All the sweetness of English showers and sunshine is mixed up with such a scene.

The cowslips come next, the cowslips which Izaak Walton loved. Probably the first fishing you ever did is marked in memory by cowslips – you were fishing for trout with a worm, and you grew tired of it and made cowslip-balls instead. Another flower of childhood is the buttercup ('Do you like butter? you said, holding it under somebody's chin; and he liked butter if the rich yellow was reflected upwards from the flower). And how exciting it was, when you ran down to the river, to find your shoes covered with golden pollen, as if the fairies had touched them. Perhaps they had.

FISHERMEN'S BIRDS

The jolly little moorhen half-angers us sometimes, when we mistake his splashing for the rise of a fish, but the waterside would be unfamiliar without him, and we should be sorry to miss the amusing sight of his curious waggle-tail progress across the river, and the highly improper way in which he bobs his behind as he swims. His cousin the coot is less abandoned, has less of the air of a rather entertaining gigolo, and is a more serious person altogether, with the appearance of having somewhat prematurely aged.

He and the moorhen, though they may tease us sometimes with their splashing, are the fisherman's friends, and so are all other birds that fly and swim – always excepting, of course, the odious swans, the tame ducks, the heron, the cormorant, and the shag. The pert little dabchick amuses us with his clever diving; the russet-brown water-rail delights us when we catch a glimpse of him, because he is such a skulking, secret fellow and so rarely seen; the bittern, tall, speckled, strange, thrills us with his foghorn booming from broadland reed-beds in the spring.

Then there are the wild ducks – the swift, darting teal, and the high-flying widgeon that dip and whir above the water, and whose wild whistling seems, as we make our way home after pike-fishing on cold winter nights, to come shrill and chilly from the neighbourhood of the frozen stars; the mallard that swing round and round the pool when we are fishing for bream and tench at dusk on summer evenings, that glide down across the sunset with an astonishing thunder of many wings; and the sheldrake and shelduck, sitting outside the rabbit-holes in which they build their nests, and later conducting the companies of their offspring on their first diving expeditions across the river.

In the winter, if we are lucky, we may sometimes see the wild geese. They come riding high on the winds at evening, like witches on their broom-sticks, a V-shaped convoy, heralding the rough goose-weather with their weird honk-honking which seems at first to come from nowhere out of the sky.

Then there are the gulls, which, when they fly far inland, are messengers of wild weather too; the curlew, perhaps the most loved of fishermen's birds because it is always associated in memory with the high hills and the moorlands and the little trout leaping, and because its cry in the breeding season is the queerest and the wildest and the loveliest of all; the snipe, who 'drum' so strangely at the time when we are catching our first trout on the dry-fly, and who at other seasons rise up from the rushes with a sound like a harsh cough and go zigzagging away like brown leaves on the winds; the sandpipers with their merry whistling, and the smart white-breasted oyster-catchers; the green plovers performing astonishing aerobatics and crying so sadly over the water-meadows at evening; that handsome, exotic fellow, the great crested grebe, who rules over certain ponds and lakes like some outlandish foreign potentate, who wears a strange headdress, and who speaks a very strange tongue, sometimes saying 'yicker, yicker', and sometimes exclaiming 'hick, hick'.

Loveliest of all, of course, there is the kingfisher, the rainbow's son and heir, who appears and disappears so swiftly as he darts down the river that one has the feeling that all the beauty in the world has been suddenly revealed to one and as suddenly withdrawn. (Thus fly the Muses!) That angler would be churlish indeed who would grudge a few bleak and minnows to a piece of flying turquoise with a bright red breast.

So much for the bigger birds of the waterside. There are also, just as loved and just as familiar, those smaller feathered entities – the little bundles of feathers-and-song which hop from reed-stem to reed-stem or flutter about from twig to twig in the willows. There is the chiff-chaff, who on hot and weary days almost, but not quite, tempts the catapult out of the fishing-bag, because his two notes endlessly repeated tend to become irritating and take on the savour of mockery. There are the sedge-warbler and the reed-warbler, two drab-coloured lively chatterers who reside in England only during the summer months, and the reed-bunting, much commoner than they, who lives with us all the year round and stutters out his awkward little song incessantly from March till the last days of August; the wagtails, pied, yellow, and grey, delicious perky things bobbing and strutting at the water's edge; and the dipper with his white shirt-front and his air of being extremely busy among the stones.

More scarce is the marsh-warbler, which is difficult to distinguish from the reed-warbler except by his song, a far more fluent melody than the reed-warbler's babbling; and scarce too, except in Norfolk and Devon, is the black-moustached, bearded titmouse, a very hidalgo of a bird. The marsh-tit, which resembles the coal-tit except that the nape of its neck is black instead of white, haunts streamsides and marshy places, and often makes its mossy, hair-lined nest in a hole in an old willow.

HINTS AND RECIPES

Modern Practice

BREAD PASTE

Take a slice of stale bread, remove the crust, and thoroughly soak the crumb in water. Squeeze out the water, and work into a paste. It should be fairly stiff, but not too stiff to prevent the hook penetrating when a fish is struck.

To this foundation may be added flour (which makes a stiffer paste), sugar, honey, or cheese. Honey paste is said to be good for carp, and cheese paste is certainly attractive to chub. Plain bread paste is most frequently used by roach-fishermen.

Some anglers prefer their pastes coloured red (by the addition of vermilion) or yellow (by the addition of chrome yellow). Others flavour with aniseed. We mistrust such devices, but they may have their use in keeping the angler's heart up when the fish won't bite. To make paste by the waterside, wrap a slice of bread-crumb in a piece of clean linen, soak well, and knead for several minutes, keeping the bread inside the linen all the time. See that your hands are clean and do not smell of tobacco.

The size of the piece of paste used on the hook varies from a piece as big as a hazel-nut to a fragment smaller than a pea. Generally speaking, use a big piece for coloured water, a small one for clean water.

Much-fished-for roach are apt to fight shy of the usual pear-shaped piece. It might be worth while to vary the shape occasionally.

BREAD-CRUST

Cut thin strips, half crust, half crumb, from the outside of a stale loaf, cover the strips with a damp cloth and press them between two boards with a heavy weight on top, leaving them thus for several hours. Then cut the strips into small dice-like cubes. They will swell in the water, so should be on the small side when cut. Keep in a tin box. To bait, insert the point of the hook in the *crust* and bring it out through the *crumb*. It should protrude very slightly.

BOILED WHEAT, MALT AND BARLEY

Boiled Wheat. Soak in water for a few hours, then let it simmer over a fire until the grains begin to burst and the white pith shows. To bait insert the hook through the husk and bring out through the soft part. Wheat may, with advantage, be boiled in milk instead of water.

The week-end angler may find it convenient to use this method. Put the wheat in a thermos flask to one-third of its capacity and fill up with boiling water. Leave for about three hours, and the wheat will be fully cooked.

Malt is prepared in the same way as wheat, but takes twice as long to stew.

Pearl Barley should be boiled until it is soft.

HEMP-SEED

To prepare hemp put half a pint of seed into a small saucepan half-filled with water and boil slowly on a gas-ring. When boiling-point is reached, lower the gas and let the hemp simmer until the seed bursts and the white germ protrudes.

Hemp turns sour very quickly and will not keep for more than a day or two.

BULLOCK'S PITH AND BRAINS

To prepare this bait (one of the best for chub-fishing in the winter) cut the *pith* (which is the spinal marrow of an ox) into pieces about the size of a hazel-nut, having first removed the outer skin and washed the pith until it is white. Use it on a six or eight hook, threaded and worked up the shank. The *brains* are used as groundbait. They should be boiled for about an hour in a calico cloth, and mashed or minced before use.

Groundbaits

For Roach. The purpose of groundbaiting is to lure the fish to the swim and to give them an appetizer rather than a feed. 'Cloud' groundbaits (used chiefly for roach) are those which disintegrate on being cast into the water and dissipate in the form of little milky clouds. Heavier groundbaits (often mixed with balls of clay) are used for bottom-feeding fish such as bream and barbel. The groundbaits most frequently used are: *pulped bread, bread and bran, 'cloud' groundbait* (such as powdered bread, condensed milk and sugar), *chopped worms and gentles, hemp* (which should be used very sparingly).

For Rudd. Half a loaf of bread attached to a small stone by a piece of string, so that it is anchored just beneath the surface.

For Bream. Brewers' grains, lobworms (chopped up) in clay balls, bread and bran, boiled wheat and raw wheat (mixed), barley-meal and ground-up greaves (mixed).

For Barbel. Greaves; bread, bran and barley-meal (mixed), lobworms (groundbaiting with lobs is an expensive proceeding, as sometimes four thousand or more are used to bait one swim, and the dose repeated two or three mornings before the fishing).

For Tench. Bran with greaves, middlings, stewed wheat, or bread, to which a few chopped worms are added.

For Carp. Bran, barley-meal and stale bread, in lumps about the size of a tennis ball.

The following recipes may be found useful as a guide to the preparation of these groundbaits:

1 BREAD GROUNDBAIT

Take several pounds of stale bread, soak in cold water for an hour, drain off water, and pulp the bread thoroughly. Squeeze into small balls and throw into the swim when required.

2 BREAD AND BRAN GROUNDBAIT

Using (1) as a foundation, add a peck of bran, and work the whole into a stiff mixture. Make up into balls about the size of an orange.

3 MIXED BREAD GROUNDBAITS

Using (1) or (2) as a foundation, add boiled rice, brewers' grains, or Thorley's cattle food; *or* gentles, hempseed, or chopped worms, according to the hook bait which is to be used.

John, aged about three, in the courtyard of Tudor House. In the background is the ancient studded door mentioned in *Portrait of Elmbury*.

John and Daphne Moore, aged six and four.

(*above*) John and Daphne aged 18 and 16, (*right*) John in 1944 and (*below*) John and Lucile after their wedding at Caxton Hall, 1 April 1944.

4 CLOUD GROUNDBAIT

Cut a loaf in two, remove crust, dry the two slices in an oven, rub or grind into a powder, add a little condensed milk and fine sugar, and mix well. Damp the powder by the waterside, as needed. Ground biscuits may be added; and silver sand is sometimes used to make the bait sink in swift water.

5 BRAN AND BARLEY-MEAL

For Bream.   Knead together broad flaky bran, fresh barley-meal, and stale bread well soaked in water. Use in lumps the size of a tennis ball.

For Carp.   Insert three or four small, skinned, par-boiled potatoes in each lump.

6 VARIATIONS OF ABOVE

Using (5) as a foundation (without the potatoes), add brewers' grains, raw or boiled wheat, ground-up greaves and oil-cake, singly or in combination. Clay may be added to stiffen the mixture and make it sink.

7 GREAVES

For Barbel.   Cut the greaves into lumps about an inch square and soak thoroughly. Mix with clay if necessary, or with bread, bran and barley-meal.

8 LOBWORMS

For Barbel and Bream.   Mix with lumps of clay, and use either chopped or whole. *Or* procure some small, thin, brown-paper bags, tear off the bottom corners of each bag, making a hole about the size of a florin, and stop each hole with a stone. Then fill up the bag with lobworms, screw up the top, and drop quietly into the swim. The bags will soon disintegrate and the worms be distributed about the eddy by the currents.

AN OLD POACHER'S METHOD OF GROUNDBAITING

In summer-time, tie a sheep's head to the end of a pole and fix the pole so that it projects over the swim. The maggots which fall from the sheep's head will attract the fish to the swim; but they may also fall upon the heads of romantic young couples in boats who have chosen that very backwater for their love-making. Therefore this method is not recommended to the tender-hearted.

HINTS

TO MAKE A ROD-REST

Cut two forked twigs from a willow-tree, each about catapult size. One should have a handle about a foot long, the other need not have a handle at all. Insert the handle of the one in the ground, rest the rod in its fork, and peg down the butt of the rod with the fork of the other.

TO STRAIGHTEN GUT

Draw it three or four times through a slit in a cork or between a piece of india-rubber folded and pressed tightly between the thumb and forefinger.

To *dull gut*, rub it with dock leaves; to *de-grease gut*, pass it to and fro through a handful of dead bracken; to *sink gut*, in wet-fly fishing, anoint it with glycerine or rub it with clay.

A SUBSTITUTE FOR A MINNOW

Should you find yourself in the position of possessing an Archer tackle, but no fish wherewith to bait it, take two strips of willow and place these together upon the flight so that the one side shows olive and the other white. This will spin quite well and will take fish.

SUBSTITUTES FOR A FLOAT

If you have left your float at home, do not be discouraged; make shift with a twig, a match-stick, or the cork from your beer bottle. If the fish are shy, these substitutes may be better than the original. A water-lily leaf makes an excellent float when fishing for shy carp; if there is a breeze it acts as a sail, carrying the bait right out into the middle of the lake, and it is less likely to be suspected by the fish than anything else.

LOBWORMS AND EELS

You will probably get just as much fun in catching your lobworms the previous night as you will with the bream next day. Catching lobworms is one of the great Outdoor Sports. It is the most hilarious game in the world. You take a lantern each – half a dozen of you – and with bent backs you creep over the lawn, where the worms are lying out on the grass; but you have to be uncommonly quick and silent, or they will elude you when you make your grab at them. They will hear you coming and be down their holes like scared rabbits. And when you have got one, hold him firmly, or he will slip out of your fingers; and if he is half-way down his hole already, you must pull very gently to get him out, for he has a nasty habit of coming in two. Lobworms lie out on the grass most plentifully after rain; but if the season is dry you can deceive them by an application of the garden hose, just before dusk.

An average bag for a beginner is two lobworms in an hour. If the lawn possesses hazards in the form of croquet-hoops the bag may be only one; you trip up and lose your temper. Everybody else laughs. But after much practice you become expert. One day, perhaps, you may write a treatise on lobworm-hunting, and so achieve immortality.

A lesser sport, also subsidiary to bream-fishing, is that of removing from the hook any eels who have swallowed the worm which was intended for the bream. This is a sport (similar to that of watching wretched animals walking about cages at the Zoo) which is only entertaining to the onlookers. To the principal it is not sport. It is said that men can be divided into two classes: those who can stop a dog-fight, and those who can't. It might have been said that they can also be divided thus: those who keep their dignity when dealing with an eel, and those who don't. I am of the latter.

The Angler's Weekend Book

My old Colonel, whose green deerstalker was practically feathered by the enormous number of flies which he'd stuck in it, used to be the owner of this stream. He was a man who despised nothing that was shootable, catchable, or conceivably eatable; and I have told[1] how he spent half a day fishing for minnows to make minnow-tansy as described by Izaak Walton, and how he fished for eels on Sunday afternoons, using half a dozen rods each with a little bell attached to them; so that the bells awakened him out of a whisky-slumber whenever there was a bite. The forked withies which he stuck in the bank to make rod-rests have mostly taken root, and are now big trees leaning across the stream; his green and lovely and living memorial. But they have made the stream more difficult to fish than ever. The Colonel, who was the best angler I ever knew, used to tie a horsehair cast to the top joint of his fly-rod – he was surely the last man to use horsehair – and lying on his belly, crawling among the nettles, swear-

[1] *Come Rain Come Shine.*

ing, grunting, blowing like a grampus, would flick his mayfly into apparently-unreachable places, out of which he took trout weighing up to two pounds.

His rod was as old-fashioned as he was; it was made of greenheart, and it had been frequently broken and wonderfully spliced. Waxed thread of many different colours was whipped round the splices. The top had a permanent kink in it, due I dare say to the quantity of heavy fish which it had landed. Bearing this rod jauntily down the river, the old Colonel would describe it as 'My old weapon'. Then he'd give me one of his wicked grins. 'It's seen a lot of service, you see. My old weapon.'

He possessed another rod which was too long and heavy to use in the little brook, and this one had a curious history. It was supposed to have belonged to J.W.M. Turner, who used it when he fished the famous Houghton Club water on the Test. How it had come into the Colonel's hands I don't know; but he was very proud of it on the grounds of its antiquity and associations.

'Belonged to J.W.M. Turner,' he used to say. 'Painting feller, wasn't he?' He didn't know anything else about him, and if he had ever seen it I'm sure he would have likened the 'Sun Rising Through Vapour' to a fried egg. But nevertheless he seemed to feel that the rod had acquired some special virtue from its previous owner, and he only used it on special occasions, such as when the mayfly was up on his favourite Cotswold river. Once he allowed me to fish with it. His own arm was tired, I think; for the barge pole of a rod was 14 foot long and entirely out of balance – it had a tiny little reel without a ratchet, which had also been Turner's, and it was so top heavy that my line made a splash every time it hit the water. No wonder I didn't catch a trout with it, although the flies were coming downstream like flotillas of miniature sailing boats and the river was dappled with rises, a black blunt snout in the middle of every ripple-ring. That was about nine o'clock in the evening; the sun was going down behind the willows, and suddenly a mist came up and crept stealthily over the willows, thickened into whiteness, and became streaked with orange; so that for a minute or two I saw what Turner had seen, and felt I was in the presence of a ghost – of him whose hand had gripped the butt of that great rod, whose hand had guided the camel-hair brush across the wet paper.

I have another reason to remember this particular day's fishing in the Colonel's company; for during the afternoon he gave a remarkable demonstration of the enterprise, determination and sheer ruthlessness which possessed him when he was in pursuit of any kind of game. The trout, satiated with mayflies, suddenly stopped rising; and the Colonel took it into his head that the only fly which might tempt them was a Greenwell's Glory. He rummaged in vain through his fly-box – there were Wickham's Fancies, Tup's Indispensables, Red Spinners, Blue-winged Olives, Gold-ribbed Hare's Ears, Welshman's Buttons, March Browns – but never a Greenwell, though it was the Colonel's favourite fly. He took off his deerstalker hat and sought among the old, weather-beaten flies which practically thatched the top of it; but he couldn't find a Greenwell there. Never mind; he would tie himself one. So he stumped off to a farmyard, which happened to be nearby, whence shortly I heard a loud cackling and squawking. He returned in triumph, having despite his arthritis overtaken and fallen upon a suitable cockerel, and plucked from its neck the appropriate hackle feather – red-brown with black tips. He now took out of his pocket the catapult which he always carried out fishing (for the purpose of driving away swans, which he hated) and chose from the streamside a well-worn stone. Then, with the catapult at the ready, he crept down a hedgerow; and within a quarter of an hour he had shot himself a cock blackbird. With two of its smoky wing-feathers, the cock's hackle, and a hook out of his hat he soon tied a passable imitation of the fly which is named after a sporting parson, Canon Greenwell, whose 'Glory' it was to fill a basket of trout with it at Kelso in 1852. The Colonel put this fly on his cast, and looking very angry, which he always did when engaged in the chase, he crawled upstream, found a good fish rising, threw the Greenwell over it, and landed a two pounder. And he had another to match it before that evening mist came up, and ended our fishing.

Man and Bird and Beast

Although one could never condone the shooting of a blackbird – be it cock or hen – one cannot but admire the Colonel's ingenuity!

IZAAK WALTON

You can go a-Maying in English literature and find there many a sweet spring morning – there is one in *The Prologue,* full of elvish laughter, there are some in Shakespeare's songs, there are dancing daffodils in Michael Drayton, there are hawthorn sprigs in Herrick; but when you come to *The Compleat Angler* your search will be ended, for there is a book that is the whole spring. It has the very air and spirit of those cowslip days, it possesses all the showers and the shadows and the sunshine of May. It goes into your pocket whole, unscissored, unabridged; and in your pocket you have all England and all the spring.

Andrew Lang said charmingly that it was 'a book to be marked with flowers, marsh-marigolds and fritillaries, and petals of the yellow iris', and I do not doubt that its pages have frequently held such pleasant hostages to memory. Apart from the virtues of its good, sound Elizabethan prose, its kindliness, its spring-morning beauty, it has a certain limited practicality as well; and therefore it has probably been read as often by the waterside as in the study. Doubtless it has been used many times for the purpose of storing flies and gut-casts, has fallen into the water and been rescued with the landing-net, has shared the fishing-basket with a brace of trout or chub. These adventures make it unique as a book, just as angling, which is 'somewhat like poetry' is unique as a sport. Hunting, if we except the erudition of Peter Beckford and the sweet wistfulness of Sassoon's *Foxhunting Man,* has always been associated with a sort of hearty unliterariness; shooting has produced nothing very memorable either in poetry or prose. It is left to angling, the queerest sport that man ever devised, to flirt with the things of the mind and to give birth, astonishingly, to this delicious piece of riverside literature, in which the very may-flies come alive and go dancing over the eddies, in which there are English flowers and meadows, there are cowslips, there is May.

Yet all anglers are not so sensitive. The only contemporary criticism of Walton's book which we may still read is contained in a book written by Richard Franck, himself a fisherman. This Franck was a trooper of Cornwall, a Northerner, a dull pedantic fellow, and probably a sour one; for who could ride with men who possessed such names as Praisegod Barebones and still keep his sense of humour? At any rate, Franck had nothing but contempt for *The Compleat Angler.* He called it an 'indigested octavo', pitied Walton for his credulity, accused him of plagiarism, and hinted that he knew very little about angling.

Now the temper of Cromwell's men was so dismal – or the historians have made it appear so – that it would really be surprising if one of them saw any beauty in anything; they preferred to cast their eyes downwards, looking cheerlessly for hellfire. And perhaps this was the reason why Franck failed to notice the sunshine in Walton's book and saw only the inaccuracy and the superstition. Also, we must remember that Walton was on the side of the King. If Franck was not prejudiced at least he had good cause to be so. On the one occasion when these two met, at Stafford, and Walton 'huffed away' because Franck teased him about his ridiculous pet theory, that pikes were bred out of pickerel-weed, there was possibly another and a stronger reason for disagreement, if Walton happened to mention King Charles.

Nevertheless – though this is heresy – I am inclined to believe that Walton was not a very expert fisherman after all. Franck was; he caught salmon and trout in the Esk, and in the swift dangerous northern streams. Old Izaak's methods were antiquated even for those times; he had probably never used a reel, he knew nothing at all about salmon, he had probably never wielded a fly-rod, and he stole his list of flies from his mysterious predecessor, Dame Juliana Berners, who wrote the *Treatyse of Fysshynge wyth an Angle*. But what must have shocked Franck most of all was Walton's concern with the small fry, the trivial side-lines of fishing. Like an urchin with a bent pin, he was content to spend long afternoons fishing for little dace and gudgeon. To Franck he must have seemed an amateur indeed! Never to have felt the first thrilling terrible rush of a salmon in a swift river! Never to have raced downstream praying that the line might hold while a clean-run fish leaped again and again at the end of it! And yet boldy to assert the gudgeons and bleaks and daddy-ruffs were 'excellent fish', and to be content to angle for them! No wonder Franck was contemptuous. It is very hard, when you have once fished for salmon, to believe that anything else is worth fishing for; you have to be something of a poet, or a whimsical fellow like Hugh Sheringham. I, who am neither, have been guilty these last two years of making a solemn vow, in the train between Perth and Crewe, that never again would I wet a line except in the cause of salmon or trout; and if you call me a snob I must remind you that even kindly Andrew Lang remarked that 'a bait-fisher *may* be a good man, as Izaak was, but it is easier for a camel to pass through the eye of a needle'.

Franck probably held the same opinion. Remember also that he was a Parliament man, unlikely to be well-disposed towards a Royalist; that he was a practical-minded person, whereas Izaak was highly superstitious; and finally that he did not understand that angling was 'somewhat like poetry' – and, making these allowances, perhaps we can excuse him for being unmoved by Izaak's May morning, perhaps we can even forgive his unkind words about the 'indigested octavo'.

It is rather strange that so quiet a harvest as *The Compleat Angler* should have come out of such unquiet times. While Izaak was planning and writing his book England was at civil war. On more than one of his fishing days Izaak must have heard the clatter of hoofs on the bridge and left his float unwatched while he cheered the plumed cavaliers or frowned at those other soldiers, the queer, sour fellows who sang hymns and fought for Parliament. But the hymn-singers won, and Charles, condemned a murderer and a traitor, lost his head and gained his martyrdom.

Four years later, when Cromwell was unmaking one Parliament and making another, a Parliament of Saints with weird names, Izaak's undistinguished-looking eighteenpenny octavo first saw light in a troubled world. Within the next twelve years, which witnessed the Restoration, the Plague, the Fire, and the Dutch raid on the Medway, it ran through five editions; so even in those stirring times the may-fly did not forget to come out, and 'anglers, honest men' still had leisure to concern themselves with it. Izaak himself must have seen many strange events, but he had not the inquisitiveness of Pepys, and he preferred fishing to sightseeing. Perhaps, however, on the famous night when the King came to his own again he forgot his fishing and his scholarship for a few hours and, casting aside his piety, took part in the most magnificent debauch in England's history. Andrew Lang, whom I must quote for a third time, remarks pleasantly: 'If Izaak were so eccentric as to go to bed sober on that glorious twenty-ninth of May, I greatly misjudge him.' I echo that kindly sentiment, and add the guess that his roystering young friend, Charles Cotton, called for him and took him off mafficking, and brought him home very drunk indeed. Next day the may-fly would be up, and they could cool their heads at the riverside!

Izaak was in London during the Plague year, and he may also have seen the Fire; but he did not write any account of these things and went quietly on with his work, collaborating with Cotton in the revised *Compleat Angler* and finishing his *Lives*. If he had been a diarist like Pepys, a student of the ways of men instead of the ways of fish, he would have been a profitable source to the historians; for he lived during five reigns: Elizabeth, James I, Charles I, the Commonwealth, and Charles II. He was born at Stafford in 1593 and he died in December

1683 at the very remarkable age – for his time – of ninety. He lived for the most part in London, and practised the trade of an ironmonger. In spirit, however, he was no small tradesman; he should really have been a cleric. He had a simple faith, unshaken by the speculations of his age, and in a country parsonage (with a mile of river as part of the glebe!) he would have been as happy as the day was long. His simplicity in religious matters were altogether delightful, and somewhat surprising in the age of such men as Donne. Writing of Dr Nowel, another Dean of St Paul's, he expresses his own faith perfectly. 'And the good old man, though he was very learned, yet knowing that God leads us not to Heaven by many, nor by hard questions, made that good, plain, unperplexed catechism which is printed with our good old Service-book.' Mark that *though he was very learned*. He always kept his respect for scholarship, but said in effect: 'I am a poor simple man, and I do not understand intricate things; you are wise and you may speculate as much as you like as long as you leave me a plain, simple faith which is within my understanding.' Izaak's ignorance was the sort of ignorance which is very, very wise. The soap-box orators of today would do well to imitate it.

It is characteristic of Izaak's religious simplicity that he takes great pains to seek commendation of his favourite sport in the Scriptures. He zealously hunts through the Bible for fish-hooks, and is almost pathetically pleased when he finds them. 'Let me tell you,' he declares, 'that in the Scripture, angling is always taken in the best sense.' Then he gives a long list of divines who have found their pleasure in angling. 'Let me add this more', he writes contentedly. 'He that views the ancient ecclesiastical canons, shall find hunting to be forbidden to clergymen, as being a turbulent, toilsome, perplexing recreation; and shall find angling allowed to clergymen, as being a harmless recreation, a recreation that invites them to contemplation and quietness.'

Country Men

SHOOTING

*The watching so often stayed the shot
that at last it grew to be a habit*

RICHARD JEFFERIES

John was a proficient shot, and also a good naturalist (the two do not inevitably go together). These gifts enhanced each other in his enjoyment.

As with fishing, the pleasures of his humble rough shoot were as great to him as the fashionable shoots which he attended on occasion, and which, I think, with the massacre of reared birds on a large scale, he probably inwardly deplored.

Though a dyed-in-the-wool wildfowler in his earlier years, when he went to live at his Mill House and kept waterfowl of many varieties, including, of course, the universal mallard, he became more interested in studying their habits and less infatuated with the slaying of their wild brethren; and towards the end of his life stopped taking part in duck-shooting expeditions.

When I became sixteen I was given a Game Book for my birthday. It was a proper Rich Uncle's present, handsomely bound in calf, gilt-edged. Each page was ruled in columns headed 'Date', 'Rendezvous', 'Host', with six more headings for recording the bag, 'Pheasants', 'Grouse', 'Partridges', 'Hares', 'Rabbits', 'Various'. There was also a space for 'Remarks'; it was indeed a lordly Game Book, a small-scale and earthly version of the kind of volume we may suppose the Recording Angel to possess – seven columns for the Deadly Sins, and a spare one for the 'Various' which would surely be needed nowadays.

On the day following my birthday I went shooting almost certainly because I wanted to make an entry in my Game Book; and I subsequently recorded that I shot one rabbit on Westmancote Farm, my host being Farmer Jackson. Ill-written with a pen accustomed to doing Lines, which spluttered on the thick matt paper, this record didn't seem much to boast about; for I felt one should really have been in the position, as the owner of such a fine book, to put 'Lord Blank' as one's host, '101 pheasants, 30 partridges, 15 hares' as one's bag (no 'rabbits'!) and, under Remarks, some such laconic comment as 'His Excellency shot well'.

However, I had made a start; and next day I was able to write proudly '1 various' in the column provided for the purpose. The 'Rendezvous' was 'Withy Bed'. Nothing is entered under 'Host' so I assume the Withy Bed was common land or, more likely, that I had been poaching.

The various was a moorhen. It was sacrificed, I suspect, simply to satisfy my ambition to record a Various.

What creatures properly come into the category? Pigeons, wildfowl, snipe, woodcock, coots – and in Scotland black game, ptarmigan, capercailzie, roedeer. I see that I stretched a point to include 'pike 5 lbs' – fairly I think, since I shot it as it basked on the surface of a lake in September. It is one of the pleasing qualities of Various that they are generally unexpected: a wild duck gets up from a pool in a wood you are pheasant-shooting, a snipe zigzags in front of the guns as they walk a rough field for partridges, a blackcock finds its way into the bag during a grouse-drive. Various are much more exciting than normal game. One woodcock is worth a hundred pheasants in any shooting-man's life. As for the capercailzie that came noisily towards me out of a larch-wood in Aberdeenshire, crashing through snow-laden branches, it is as huge as a turkey in retrospect; indeed it has taken on the lineaments of a bird of fable, perhaps a roc or a phoenix, and I can't remember what it really looked like nor altogether believe that it fell to my 12-bore; but there it is, indisputable, in the 'Various' column of my Game Book.

There's a roebuck too. I would never shoot one again; everybody shouted, and my gun went up willy-nilly, and the finger on the trigger was automatic, unthinking. It is the least-to-be-proud-of among the Various. But what a multitude of sins the term could cover: foxes in a hunting country, poaching cats, tame ducks mistaken by the short-sighted for wild ones, dogs mistaken for hares – even beaters, in the days when it was their own damsilly fault if they didn't keep out of the way . . .

My first concern when out shooting with strangers is to avoid becoming a Various myself. I don't know how many people are killed, maimed or blinded every year by fools with guns, but when I observe the behaviour of untaught shooters I am only surprised that the casualties are not counted in thousands. Mr Douglas Service in his *Introduction to Shooting* described 'a man who pushed his gun in front of him through a hedge with the muzzle pointing towards his own body and another who finished off a hare with the stock of his gun, while the muzzle pointed at his stomach'. I knew one such character who, meeting me on the road one evening as he walked back from pigeon-shooting, told me a long funny story and emphasized its point by prodding the muzzle of his gun into the pit of my stomach. Suddenly a pigeon came over, and the man put his gun up and shot it dead. 'Lucky I kept my cartridges in,' he said.

Opinions differ concerning the best way of dealing with fellow-guests who handle their guns carelessly. The Colonel, whenever he was menaced or thought he was likely to be, would advance upon the offending one with moustaches bristling and face fire-red. 'Sir: if you dare to do that again I shall *shoot back at you*, with *both* barrels.' A more tactful course is recommended by Sir Ralph Payne-Gallway, who wrote *Letters to Young Shooters*. He enjoins his reader, in succinct if inelegant prose:

'Go home to write important letters, for 'twere better to run the risk of giving offence than to be liable to have your eyesight damaged, or even to be made a sieve of.'

When I was about six I had a popgun. I pointed it at my sister for the excellent reason that I was pretending to be a Uhlan, one of those German cavalrymen who at that time were overrunning Belgium and committing Atrocities. I didn't know what Atrocities were, but I gave the best imitation I could. I stood my sister against the wall and aimed at her forehead. Pop! The cork flew out and fell harmlessly at the end of its string. But just then my father came in. He was so angry that I thought I had really committed an Atrocity. He took the popgun away, and he made me learn by heart the rhyme:

> *Never, never, let your gun*
> *Pointed be at anyone,*
> *That it may unloaded be*
> *Matters not the least to me . . .*

and so on.

Nobody, alas, teaches those verses to the children in our village whose doting mothers or fathers give them airguns which are quite capable of blinding a human being at a range of thirty yards. It makes me hopping mad when I see little Tommy in his coonskin cap pointing his airgun at me from behind the bushes. His imagination has made one of those wonderful flights that only a child's is capable of, and he sees me as a Red Indian. 'Bang! You're dead,' says Tommy. One day somebody may be. Tommy, grown up, may pick up a twelve-bore which some fool has left loaded; he may point it at his girl and pull the trigger in fun. Bang, you're dead.

Apart from being dangerous, airguns in the hands of wanton boys are extremely destructive. You have to be a good shot to bring down a bird with a catapult; but any child, unless he's half-blind, can get a bird into the sights of a gun rested on a gate, and be pretty sure of hitting it from a range of twenty yards. The airgun makes slaughter far too easy, and I know very well that when three small boys, all provided with airguns, pass my house on their way up Brensham Hill, at least a dozen songsters are likely to become casualties before long. Boys possessing weapons do *not* go in for competitive target practice at, let us say, old tins. They prefer a living target; and I'd be a prig if I blamed them for that. Between seven and sixteen I was rarely without a catapult; and the only inanimate object I ever took pleasure in shooting at was a police station window, which I broke. For the rest my sport was provided by unfortunate water-rats, as they passed upon their lawful occasions from one bank of the Avon to the other, and by numerous birds, ranging in size from sparrows to pigeons. *But*, remember, you have to be a good shot to hit a bird with a catapult; no boy, however skilful, is likely to hit very many, and most of those will be the tamer and common kinds. Airguns on the other hand are lethal enough, and are becoming plentiful enough, to do real harm to the fauna. But few parents care about this, and even if they did they are such softies that they would not dare deny little Tommy his gun. They are even prepared to take the risk of him shooting somebody's eye out, after all.

Man and Bird and Beast

That curious little book which we had as children, *Eyes and No Eyes*, helped to educate John's already unusually discerning eye, and this stood him in good stead in later years. Taking a shoot 'on the strength of a tiny curled up feather' showed immense faith and acute observation, and what he described as this 'flimsy bit of evidence' paid off handsomely in the years to come. I asked a country-loving friend – a notable shot – whether he, too, would have risked disappointment on such a slender clue, and he readily agreed that he would, in similar circumstances, have done just that.

THE MARSH

I took Eli's shoot on the strength of a tiny, curled-up feather, no more substantial than a piece of blown thistle-down, which I found floating at the edge of one of the puddles in the Marsh. It was a flimsy bit of evidence; but it had come from the breast of a wild duck that had paddled about in the slop looking for food, and where one duck had fed it was likely that there would be more. So I went to see Eli and made an offer for the shoot, not because I believed his stories of great coveys of partridges and hundreds of pheasants, but because I wanted to stand out on that lonely and haunted-looking Marsh in the winter dusks and wait for what might come out of the sky.

The gloominess of the place was part of its fascination for me. Except in summer, when the bogs dried up and Eli's scruffy cattle pastured on the coarse grasses, it was unvisited by man or domestic beast. No house, no road, could be seen from it. Only the cries of wild things broke its silences.

On three sides of it a slow brook, joined every hundred yards or so by smaller dykes and runnels, flowed darkly through the bog. In wet seasons all these watercourses flooded and covered the whole Marsh to a depth of three or four feet. Along the banks of the main brook grew up a company of stricken goat-willows, surrounding the whole Marsh so that at dusk they looked like witches standing in a circle on the occasion of some dreadful Sabbath. Dwarfed and ancient, they held up gaunt contorted arms to the sky, as if in supplication or despair.

No merry birds ever twittered in these trees. Only the wind moaned through them and the ground at their roots made strange gurglings and chokings when you trod upon it.

Eli's Marsh was the sort of place, in fact, where a woman might be expected to wail for her demon lover under a waning moon. It was also a perfect place for geese and wild duck!

A DUCK-SHOOTING DIARY

Here is the diary of my first year's wildfowling in the Marsh:

October 30. Two or three inches of flood-water cover the whole place. This hides the dykes, and I walked straight into one of them, filling my boots with cold water. Cat-ice at the edges of the 'slop' crackled as I walked through it. At dusk it began to freeze hard.

Stamped up and down like a sentry, trying to get my feet warm. Little owls calling from the top corner – mocked them to while away the time. Then the barn owls started talking. One of them, whose voice seems to have broken, made a noise exactly like someone trying to imitate a barn owl and doing it badly. For a few minutes I thought I wasn't the only human in the Marsh!

A moorhen made unearthly sounds in one of the brooks. She cried out that she was being murdered. She yelled and screamed and hollered for help. Then she choked and coughed most horribly, pretending that something was strangling her. This is the usual play of moorhens.

Then from behind me that low purring quak-quak-quak-quak-quak. Two wild ducks slanting down together against what was left of the sunset. Of course I missed. Slanting duck are worse than planing pheasants.

Silence for a bit, then suddenly the air was full of panting wings. It was difficult to see them, for the moon was bright in a clear sky. But I got a view of three as big as mangel-wurzels above my head and the drake came down with a splash almost at my feet.

November 5. Full moon and clear sky. My mad white owl was calling again, now from my right, now from my left, now close to me, now far away. A distracted lunatic, he went round and round in an aimless circle, hurrying frantically from tree to tree. Perhaps he isn't an owl at all, but the ghost of an owl that has died.

Few duck came, and I only shot one, which flew into the moon. There seemed to be shooting going on all round me. Bangings and poppings from all over the place, so that I was quite bewildered until suddenly I remembered that it was Bonfire Night. All the village was celebrating. Now and then I saw a rocket tower heavenwards, grow bigger as it mounted to the stars, and fade in despair as it found out how remote they were. Lucky Guy Fawkes! We try to think of him as a villain, but what man has a lovelier epitaph, re-written in the sky every year!

November 12–17. High floods. It is impossible to get out into the middle of the Marsh, and there on the water flocks of wild duck and teal sit all day, laughing at me. If I put them up with a shot they get off the water with a great and exciting clatter, circle until they are well out of range, and then fly over me, still laughing.

November 20. The flood is draining off and it is my turn to laugh. Got three, standing right out in the middle of the quite shallow flood-water at dusk. Duck never see you if you stand perfectly still; indeed I think it is better to be in the open than under trees, because the birds are shy of cover from which guns have so often banged at them.

November 21. They came early to-night, against a primrose sunset. They looked very black and clear-cut in the lemon-coloured light; but I missed them all the same!

December 18. The Squire, who is an angry red-faced fellow, took his son, just home for the holidays, to the Marsh at my invitation. They got some duck, but as the flood is very high, and Squire doesn't know where the dykes are, he fell in and apparently quite disappeared, except for his deer-stalker hat. I asked the boy if he swore, and got the answer, 'From the bubbles, – something awful!'

On *Christmas Day* I crept out at tea-time feeling like a conspirator (with the gun hidden under my coat) and in a high wind shot an unfamiliar duck which turned out to be a sheldrake. Later I tried to eat the thing: a remarkable experience.

January 2. Took two London friends who are staying with me. I placed them in positions where they could do no harm to each other or to me, and took myself about half a mile away. One possesses an old hammer-gun which frightens me.

Great black clouds rolling across the sky like waves in an overhead sea.

Plenty of duck, and they were easy to see (for you can see duck much more clearly against heavy clouds at night than you can by starlight). I got two widgeon, a mallard, a pochard, and a poor little tuftie (by accident). One shot from my friends.

When I joined them I asked 'What luck?' They shook their heads. 'See anything?' 'Nothing,' they said. They were very cold and wet and miserable and they had fallen into the dykes.

'But,' I said, 'I thought I heard a shot?'

The one with the hammer-gun said mournfully:

'It went off.'

'*What?* It went off?'

'Oh, it just went off.' He seemed surprised that I should think the trifling accident worth talking about at all.

January 3. To-night I lent him a hammerless gun and sent him off alone half a mile away. I swopped positions with my other friends, but although I had plenty of shooting I didn't hear a shot from anybody else.

We went back to the Hobnails afterwards, drank rum and played darts and warmed ourselves in front of Bob's huge fire. I was rather worried because I believed that my friends almost suspected me of some extraordinary cunning in putting myself where the duck were going to come and sending them to the worst places.

'Look here,' I said, 'haven't you seen a duck at all?'

They agreed: 'Not a feather.'

'Well, haven't you *heard* anything?' I asked.

It seemed they had heard a lot. They had heard the most horrible and disquieting noises. My masochistic moorhen had curdled their blood. The wind had turned itself into an invisible ghostly Something which had walked past them sighing and moaning. The mad owl had flown round them pretending to be a moonstruck mortal. Peewits had sobbed over their heads. Redshanks had wailed out of the skies. Herons had croaked at them, curlews had cried like lost souls. But of duck they had heard nothing but a distant quack or two. And what was the good of a quack, they added, when you couldn't see the author of it?

'Nothing else?' I asked.

The one whose gun had gone off by accident gave me the clue I wanted.

'There *was* another sound,' he said. 'It was like Angels Off.' (He was an actor.) 'You know, swishings and pantings and so on. But though I stared till my eyes watered I couldn't *see* anything.'

Then I realised that the duck had come to us all impartially, but my friends, who weren't used to looking for duck in a dark sky, had been actually incapable of seeing them. It's a trick which you only acquire with practice, and it's largely a matter of learning to look *in front of* the sound. It's no use staring into the sky for long periods on end; you must look down at the ground until you hear the wings and then turn your head up suddenly.

January 15.   Snow at last! I went to Miss Stevens' shop to try to buy a nightshirt; but she hadn't got a white one, so I bought a shroud instead. I tied a white handkerchief round my head and looking exactly like John Mytton in Leach's picture I stalked teal in the dykes rather successfully. I thought what a good headline it would make if I shot myself by accident. DONNED SHROUD, WALKED OUT TO DEATH. I also thought how remarkable it was that Miss Stevens should stock shrouds as well as babies' comforters. She caters for everything: our endings and our beginnings.

January 19.   And now a big flood, – the Marsh is showing me all its moods. This afternoon I brought my boat up from the river, camouflaged it with branches till it looked like Birnam Wood going to Dunsinane, and anchored it at the edge of the Marsh.

January 20.   Last night it began to freeze; all today it froze like hell. A bitter nor'-east wind, so it looks like holding. My oars tinkled through a thin scum of ice when I rowed out into the middle of the flood this evening. There was a hard silver moon in a clear sky, cold brittle-looking stars. Difficult to believe that those thousand thousand suns burn fiercer than our own!

Not a duck to be seen; but I heard the thin sad crying of widgeon which went over high out of sight, riding on the wind, and once I thought I heard the far honking of geese.

January 21.   The geese came over me and I missed them.

I can hardly bear to write about it.

I honestly believe that it is better to be crossed in love, to have chronic indigestion, to go bankrupt, to be sent to prison, than to miss clean a flock of fourteen grey lags about thirty feet above your head. Othello's, Cleopatra's, Hamlet's sorrows were as nothing to this.

I had chopped a way through inch-thick ice and placed my boat in the line of the willows, so that it looked, I hoped, just like another willow. For ages I heard nothing and saw nothing. Then I both saw and heard simultaneously. The thing I saw was a small cloud the size of a man's hand, dark against a bigger cloud, which suddenly as I watched it curled smokily out into a long line, became darker, then took to itself several pairs of wings. The thing I heard was a sound like that of a pack of hounds crying as they go up a steep wooded hill on the opposite side of a valley.

They came so quickly that they were over me almost before I had reached for my gun. I fired miles behind them – Birnam Wood got in the way – although they looked so enormous, and were so tightly packed together that it seemed almost impossible to miss them. They went on, honking furiously, and in a few seconds they were a cloud again, that melted into one of the great black clouds that were rolling down from the north.

> *There was never a story of more woe*
> *Than this of Juliet and her Romeo.*

Nonsense!

January 22.   The thaw. The wind got round to the west while I sat in the boat waiting for those geese to come back again. (Of course they didn't!) The ice began to crack with a noise like pistol shots. I had never heard the sound at night before, and didn't realise how loud it could be. Each crack was followed by the long sibilant hiss of water rushing in to fill it. Sometimes an obstinate piece of ice would creak for a long time before it broke. In the brook tiny icebergs jingled with a strange music like that made by those curious arrangements of thin glass which are hung in gardens so that they play a high faint tune when the wind catches them.

When I rowed home it sounded as if a brigade of infantry was in action with a battery of eighteen-pounders behind them.

January 23. The red-letter day: 4 teal, 3 widgeon, 5 mallard, a golden-eye, and a pochard. It had thawed for an inch or two on top of the ice, which gave the water a curious greasy appearance – it was the colour of pewter. Four sedate swans lost their dignity altogether trying to walk about on it.

The duck came in very low – looking for safe landings, trying to distinguish between the ice and the water. The sky was perfect: fleecy clouds drifting across a three-quarter moon. A north-west wind, fresh but not too noisy. All the conditions were right.

The teal came first. They flew as fast as snipe, or faster. The little parties burst like a bomb when I fired my first barrel and my second shot was always wasted. I strewed the ground at my feet with empty cartridge-cases and feathers.

Then the mallard, the golden-eye (a single bird), and the pochard, and last the widgeon, an enormous flock of them out of which I was lucky enough to kill two with one shot. They made a grand crack when they came down on the ice, and set up all sorts of crackings and creakings all over the Marsh, which continued for about five minutes!

Feburary 3. Great flocks of peewits have come to the Marsh. At night they make every conceivable sort of noise and even deceive me into thinking they are duck! They flight very low, and whizz just past my head, doing aerobatics for fun. There are very few duck now; the widgeon have gone north, and only a few mallard and teal come to the brooks in twos and threes.

February 28. The elms in the distance are wine-coloured and the Marsh is green with new grass springing. On this last night no duck came; but all my old friends were there: the little owls, the moorhen whose life seems to be one long crucifixion, the sad lunatic barn owl with the broken voice. There was a primrose sunset and a heron flew across it, looking wild and lonely and terrifically significant. Then, as the primrose faded and the sky became eggshell-blue, there came from the meadows on the left of the Marsh a new sound: the last challenging call of partridges which have settled for the night; and those partridges, I knew, were a pair.

The Countryman's England

MY SHOOT

Eli is my landlord in the matter of the Marsh Farm Shoot, which I take from him at the yearly rental of a shilling an acre on the condition – which Eli never observes – that he shall keep his pack of unruly dogs tied up or locked up on partridge-shooting days. But always the same thing happens: we toil all the hot morning to drive the partridges into a field of roots, and just as we are about to have some sport, bang through the roots goes Eli's abominable collie, with a long-dog belonging to Eli's sons and probably Old Silly-face as well (picked up from the Hobnails), away go the partridges, and that's that. It is a remarkable thing that Eli's dogs always seem to be engaged in running rapidly and purposefully about his farm. Perhaps it is something to do with his purges.*

The shoot, such as it is, includes a piece of coppice which, by comparison with the Twin Spinneys, we call the Big Wood; the Osier Bed, which is full of snipe and black mud; the Marsh itself, a good place for duck in frosty weather; the rough banks rising up on either side of the lane called Green Street; two big bare pastures, Shrew-Ash Field and the Home Ground; and a small rough feggy field called Moucher's Corner. On the other side of the road lies the Summer Leasow, through which there trickles a little winding brook, contemptuously called The Piddle. I have not marked the name on my map, but it is a genuine one, and you will find it on the Ordnance Sheet.

We always name places appropriately, calling a spade a spade. . . .

*See *The Countryman's England*, pp 89–90.

NOTE FOR DOG-TRAINERS

There is a story, which I don't altogether believe, about one of Eli's dogs, an ill-bred, ill-mannered collie which he sold to another farmer with the guarantee that it was 'perfectly trained'. Its purchaser, by way of testing this guarantee, took it out into a field and told it to lie down. It continued to run about.

'LIE DOWN!' shouted the farmer.

It took no notice at all, and began to chase his ewes, which were in yean.

When the farmer caught it he took it back to Eli and angrily demanded what the devil he meant by selling such a disobedient brute as 'perfectly trained'.

'What did you say you said to it?' asked Eli.

'I told the So-and-so to "Lie down"'

A slow smile broke over Eli's face.

'Ah,' he said. 'I see. You was wrong; you should 'a' said, "LAY DOWN."'

BEWITCHED ACRES

Of late, Eli's shoot has seemed to be bewitched. On August 31st, when I walk round without a gun, I can find a covey in almost every field; on September 1st they have vanished like smoke and four of us toil all day for a total bag of two brace. That's bad enough, but what is still more annoying is that every living thing on the farm seems to conspire, not so much to escape me as to make me ridiculous before my friends. Last September, during one of our long fruitless walks after partridges, my Labrador Benjamin got so sick of it that he ran questing down a hedge, poked his head into a patch of briar, and began to wave his tail. The man who was with me cocked his gun and there appeared suddenly from the bush two prodigious and unnatural rabbits, the one inky black and the other snowy white, and they cantered quite slowly together across our front. My friend dropped his half-raised gun and looked at me with a most pitiful expression, as if to say, 'Am I really seeing things?' He determined to settle it, and recovered himself just in time to get a nice right-and-left. 'Funny lot of wild beasts you do keep,' he said, as if my shoot were a kind of zoo.

A month later, out ferreting, we bolted and shot the most enormous tabby cat I have ever seen. She was fat, too; she had been living on my rabbits for months. Now I have got the feeling that anything may happen on Eli's farm. The thick covert at the top of the fallow may contain, for all I know, a unicorn or a green wildebeeste. The Osier Bed where we shoot snipe on frosty January days is the very place for a wart-hog or a brontosaurus.

MAGPIES IN MAY

What I may call legitimate game – pheasants and partridges and hares – is so scarce on my shoot that the competition for it between myself and various poachers is very severe. The poachers include Sam Ash, the local expert, of whom you will read more later, a neighbouring keeper, who is an adept with raisins, innumerable little owls, sly, anarchic, alien, some foxes, about six sparrow-hawks, an escaped peregrine trained in falconry, a vast brood of jays, two pairs of carrion-crows and several dozen magpies.

Therefore two or three times a week during the breeding season I take my gun and, looking as fierce as I can, walk round Eli's two hundred acres, – over the Marsh, over the Home Field, past the Osier Bed to the Twin Spinneys and across the Shrew-Ash Field to the small covert which, out of pure swank and by comparison with the little clumps of coppice, I call the Big Wood.

But I always feel a little ashamed of myself. If I let the gun off, it seems to make about ten times as much noise as it does at any other time of the year. There is a deafening explosion, like that of a few hundred tons of trinitrotoluene, and I stand somewhat abashed in the subsequent silence, aware that all the birds have ceased to sing and all the white rabbit-scuts have vanished. It is as if I had taken a pot-shot at Persephone herself.

It is different on October days, when the pheasants come high above the brown branches and the bang-bang of the guns is an exciting fusillade; or on a November morning, when scarlet coats stand against the covert, and the first hounds whimper, and hearts thud against ribs at the sound. I am a sportsman then; but not in May.

Like a fox sneaking furtively home in daylight, like an owl mobbed by tits, I creep shamefully through the bluebell-carpeted wood. A pair of magpies float down the valley with that queer, familiar flutter of their wings, commanding a mile of copse and meadow with watchful stare. They catch sight of the glint on my gun-barrels and sheer away just as I shoot. The two reports ring out in the quiet like the volley of a firing-party executing a spy on a sunny morning; but the birds are untouched, they go scurrying away with the wind of their own speed ruffling their long tails. I sometimes wonder if, subconsciously, I meant to miss them. . . .

I have a queer, sneaking regard for the rascals, and they, I think, look on me with a tolerant cynicism. Each spring I blow their nests to pieces and they go off and build again. Then, if I am lucky enough to find it, I blow that nest to pieces, and so they build a third, which I can never find. Each spring they rear a number of pied varmints like themselves, and grow fat upon the eggs of my pheasants. I set very elaborate and complicated traps for them, baited with eggs and horrible things such as rabbits' eyes and rabbits' guts, but they ignore these so contemptuously that they make me feel that in setting them I am doing an underhand and disgraceful thing. Once a keeper told me that the best bait was a hank of red wool tied to the bare trap. Inquisitiveness, he said, more than greed, would cost them their lives. But they ignored that too, and succeeded this time in making me feel a fool. They are rogues, but they are humorous rogues, like Sam Ash of whom I shall write later; and they are welcome to what they can steal.

The Countryman's England

This afternoon on the hill I saw the first woodcock of the season. In my part of the country the bird usually arrives round about the beginning of November: 'round about the twenty-first Sunday after Trinity,' as one of our sporting parsons used to put it. He would add that as soon as he began to read the Lesson from the Book of Daniel, he'd say to himself: 'I'll be letting off my gun at a woodcock before long.'

It is surely the silentest of birds. A blackbird, scared by a cat or a fox, shouts his alarm along the whole hedgerow, much to the benefit of its various inhabitants. A cock pheasant, flushed from among the bushes, kicks up a commotion which makes me jump – and Zena shy! Wild duck, flighting to their feeding-places, give the show away to the waiting gunner by their various excited cries, the teal by means of one of the shrillest whistles in wild nature, the widgeon by its loud and musical Whee-oo!, the drake mallard by its curious chuckling 'purr', his lady by her loud and hectoring 'Quark!' The whirring of partridges likewise warns the guns who wait behind the hedge:

> *Over the hedge the coveys whizz:*
> *Flickering, whickering partridges.*[1]

But the woodcock comes silent as a ghost. You *always* see it before you hear it, out shooting. Tap-tap-tap, go the sticks of the beaters against the trees. And suddenly, always unexpectedly, there's this mysterious ghost-bird flitting in dead silence among the branches; turning swiftly this way and that; dipping, dodging, like a will-o'-the-wisp appearing and disappearing, one moment coming straight at you, so that everybody shouts ''Cock! 'Cock!' – and the next second your gun is pointing where it has been, and the bird, like Romeo, is 'some otherwhere!'

The woodcock is missed more often than shot, probably because people get over-excited when they see it. We usually have a sweep on the first one, half a crown each and the winner takes the kitty. A friend of mine who recently went shooting with a big party in the Ardennes told me that the appearance of a woodcock there was the occasion for absolute frenzy, for the sweep had cost the rather rich guests the equivalent of a tenner each, and since there were a dozen guests, to shoot the first 'cock would have been like winning a small football pool. '*Bécasse! Bécasse! Vive la bécasse!*' yelled a score of voices, as the first (and only) woodcock flew down the ride, straight towards my friend; and all this shouting and excitement threw him into such a state of nerves that he missed it clean with both barrels so it was *Vive la bécasse!* indeed.

The 'cock must fly very fast, although it always seems to be 'flitting' quite slowly: a bird on migration, a few years ago, smashed the lantern of the light on Flamborough Head. Certainly it *rises* more quickly than any other bird I know, and although the subsequent flight is so silent the wings just at take-off make a sharp ripping sound, like tearing canvas. It is an odd, mysterious bird altogether, unpredictable in its appearances, sometimes breeding here, sometimes wintering,

[1]Patrick R. Chalmers.

sometimes 'looking in' for a few days in the course of migration. Its huge eye, set far back in the head, its long beak which always points earthwards during flight, its sharp wings, its silent flitting, all combine to make it the most distinctive of birds and like to none other. Its habits are odd, too – for it sometimes carries its nestlings between its thighs when in flight, holding them there with the help of its long bill. Several naturalists have witnessed this, and it is even suggested that woodcocks will carry their young from the nesting area to the feeding-grounds before they are strong enough to fly. They certainly bear them away if the nest is discovered, and I should think such a ride with the ghostly flier, dodging to and fro among the trees, must be as exciting an adventure as any young creature could hope to have – like having a go on the Big Dipper and the Chairo-plane thrown into one!

The Year of the Pigeons

When the fog comes down, as it did last week, we are suddenly strangers in a strange land. A man coming towards us, our best friend perhaps, looms up like a formidable giant. Familiar willow trees with pollarded tops become fabulous monsters, raising crooked arms in threat or supplication. The landing stage where the ferry-boat crosses our river might be the wharf of Lethe; will Styx look like this when at last we come to it, the far bank hidden, the mists swirling wraith-like over the dark water, loneliness lapping about us, and then the *plop-plop* of oars and the black prow of the boat suddenly showing?

On such a day I took my gun and went down to my little shoot in the marsh. The marsh was flooded, and the flood was frozen at the edges, having a margin of cat-ice all round it. Standing on the bank and looking outward I might have been an arctic explorer, no land between me and the Pole; for where the ice ended, the pewter-coloured water began, and beyond the water was nothing but the fog.

My sense of being utterly alone in a wild waste suddenly vanished as I heard a sound which I can only describe as *crunch-tinkle, crunch-tinkle* which puzzled me for a moment, until I realised that it had the rhythm of footsteps. A solitary poacher, somewhere in the fog, was bashing his way through the cat-ice in long waders. So I stepped into the cat-ice too, *crunch-tinkle, crunch-tinkle,* and – ah! he had heard me, for his footsteps had promptly stopped. I stopped too, and waited. After a little time I heard him again, well to my left; he was making for the bridge over the dyke so I barged through the ice and into the deeper water to head him off. Now I could hear him in the water too, a different sound, *swish-gurgle, swish-gurgle,* and of course he could hear me, coming nearer.

But we never saw each other. I had deep dykes to negotiate in the middle of the marsh, so he reached the bridge before me, and now he was on squelching land and I could hear it sucking at his boots as he made haste towards the lane. So the strange encounter ended, and I sat down on the parapet of the little bridge and waited for the duck.

The fog transformed everything, gave a queer twist of grotesquerie to every visible thing. A heron rose from the rushes, and it was like an enormous bird of fable, heraldic, huge, a Phoenix rising from the ashes. A wisp of snipe followed the bend of the brook, came whizzing out of the fog at what seemed a fantastic pace and were behind me and out of sight before I could fire. Then came a flock of teal. I heard them coming, first a kind of breathlessness of beating wings, and then a sound just like the roar of an express train. I missed them clean, and over my head the frightened flock fragmented like a shrapnel-shell. The fog teaches us how fallible our senses are; in ordinary light, *seeing* their approach, I should scarcely have heard the noise of the wings, – but when I couldn't see them, and my ears alone were in control, the wing-beats of a dozen teal were thunderous.

The duck came at last, a little flock of widgeon magnified by the fog till they looked almost as big as geese. I did not know I had hit one until I heard the crash on the cat-ice a moment after I fired; and I picked up a fine cock bird just in time before the dusk and the fog together settled down upon the marsh like the shades of Styx. I walked home by guesswork, a stranger in a strange land indeed; unseen cows moved away from me like a herd of elephants, an invisible peewit wailed like a disembodied spirit, a startled pony galloping round the field sounded like the approach of all the Four Horsemen of the Apocalypse laying waste the world. Indeed fog is a strange and lovely and mysterious thing! For once upon the Longmynd in Shropshire when the cloud lay thick upon the high top, I encountered two riders cantering together. Seeing me, giant-like as I loomed up both their horses shied, and for a fraction of a second I saw not men on horses, but two Centaurs, two huge prancing Centaurs come to life from a Greek vase. It was a moment of vision I shall never forget, something glorious and strange out of the mists of time, when all the young world was cradled in wonder.

The Season of the Year

⁓

An unaccustomed silence possesses the fields when the combines have finished. This sudden hush of September, which all countrymen known, is partly due to a falling-off in the volume of the insects' hum; mostly, I think, to the cutting of the corn. Standing corn is in perpetual motion; and as the wind ripples it there is a continual change of light and shade, and of colour too, accompanied by the small ceaseless noise of the shaking-together of the ears. This noise gets louder and the corn ripens. Last week you could hear the oats' murmur from the main road. But today! –

> Where all day long the wind would trouble
> The restless corn on the hill
> Lie the shaven fields of stubble
> Unfamiliarly still:
> Parson's Patch and the Seven Acre,
> Folly Furlong and Red Marley,
> Where we make for the corncrake
> A sanctuary in the tall barley.
> Now in vain the accustomed eye
> Looks for the sudden catspaws clawing;
> Ear misses the oats' sigh
> And the landrail's sawing.
> All is still where all was motion
> And the winds pass silently,
> As if we had reaped the ocean,
> Harvested the unharvested sea.

We shatter the silence with our shotguns. *September the First, Partridge shooting begins,* my old pocket diary used to say. (My current one only records *P.A.Y.E. week No. 52 begins*.) But we still walk the biscuit-coloured fields on the first of September.

This was the shooting the Colonel loved: walking-up partridges on hushed mornings when, as he put it, you could almost hear the mushrooms growing. So now at the end of my book let me remember him as I did at the beginning, that green-clad backbent figure beneath the deerstalker. (I believe he possessed only one other hat, a bowler of extraordinary shape, his father's probably, for it was the kind you see in Spy cartoons; the Colonel crammed it down on his grizzled head when he went to the funerals of his friends, which became more frequent as he himself grew older.)

Sweep the famous mole-catcher trots dutifully at his heels as we enter the first stubble-field and walk towards the sun. Later-rising through a white mist it hangs before us like a huge tangerine, and in its light the Colonel's red face burns like virginia creeper upon a south wall. But all the rest of him is green, the hat, the Norfolk jacket, those curious cycling trousers, the rough Harris stockings. He has only to stand still against the background of a hedge, and hey-presto he vanishes!

We walk for a hundred yards before anything happens; then a covey explodes almost beneath my feet, and the air is full of that whickering sound which for as long as I live I shall associate with the feel of the crisp stubble under my boots (rather like the feel of a new toothbrush when you run your finger along it!) and with the little scarlet pimpernel which creeps among the stubble, and with the hot smell of bruised camomile. Bang, bang, all along the line as the chittering covey flies down it; until at the farthest end of the line the banging becomes a mere popping, a toy-gun sound. Puffs of feathers still floating in the quiet air, and the dogs running forward, red setter, golden cocker, liver and white spaniel, Sweep the black Labrador. Tails waving, somebody whistling, somebody calling *seek, seek, seek*. Red setter cantering back, head held high, a fluttering in her jaws; trim little cocker pouncing on something that moves in the stubble; liver and white spaniel puzzled and zigzagging, *seek, seek, seek;* Sweep coming back to the Colonel at a smug trot, the partridge limp in his mouth, feathers in his eyes.

On firsts of September we would always start punctually at nine and walk until noon, and then it was whisky-time. The Colonel's military precision, his long experience, his habit of thirst, together brought us back to the rickyard at exactly two minutes to twelve; and he led us into the farmhouse through the big kitchen with its flagstoned floor. Here he turned out the contents of his capacious shooting-bag, in which there were sure to be some mushrooms mixed up with the partridges and cartridges and blood and feathers; toadstools too if he had found any, for 'a tot of whisky will quell 'em, me boy' should they happen to be poisonous. Unexpected things, as I told you before, were liable to come out of the Colonel's bag: a live slow worm, a dead weasel. He was a kind of kleptomaniac of the fields. Why? He liked, I think, to handle at leisure these live and dead creatures, curiosities, odds and sods, 'common objects of the countryside' as the old nature books called them. He saw a sinuous beauty in the slow worm, drew back the weasel's lip to admire its sharp little teeth. 'If I were a rabbit now, – *that'd* be what I'd see in a nightmare!' I have watched him stroking, lovingly and half-regretfully, the blue cheek-feathers of a jay he had shot: 'Charmin' little birds – pity we have to kill 'em.' There was nothing hypocritical about his regrets; but even if the jay had not been 'vermin' he would probably have shot it just the same. He was somewhat trigger-happy, quick on the draw if he saw any unfamiliar bird or beast; he fired at it in order to find out what it was. Once, out partridge-shooting, he bagged a macaw. It belonged to a rich neighbour of his who kept a private zoo. Besides being rich this man was happy-go-lucky and eccentric; his captives often escaped, or perhaps he let them go upon the whim of the moment. The macaw, squawking loudly, flew out of a hedge straight towards the Colonel, who slew it, as he said afterwards, more or less in self-defence; for he wasn't quite sure whether it came out of a whisky-bottle.

The shooting-lunch at the farmhouse went on for nearly two hours. There was always a ham from one of the Colonel's own pigs, sweet-cured in molasses flavoured with juniper and spices, the most delicious ham I have ever tasted, then there was an enormous apple-pie made with some special kind of apple, known as a Tomkins' Seedling, which nobody but the Colonel had ever heard of but which had a curious winey flavour and a firm flesh that went pinkish when it was cooked. There was also a knobbly cottage loaf, with farmhouse butter and a whole Stilton cheese. The Colonel was an expert on cheese, and he cared for his Stilton lovingly, keeping it at the proper temperature wrapped in a cloth which was damped slightly from time to time; he never, as the barbarians do, spoilt its flavour by pouring into it beer or stout or port. It was one of his pet theories that you could equate civilization with cheese; and that whether by coincidence or by favour

John Moore

John with Candy, his specially loved cat, in about 1954 and (*below*) Lower Mill Farm.

of heaven only those nations were truly civilized that had devoted themselves successfully to the arts of the dairy. Of course the English came out on top, having Stilton, Cheddar, Cheshire, Double Gloucester, Blue Vinny and Wensleydale, but the Colonel allowed that the French and Italians, although foreigners, ran us pretty close with their Camembert and Gorgonzola; the Swiss too, for the sake of Gruyère, though they lost a few marks for selling 'processed' cheeses wrapped in silver paper. But the rest were nowhere. Whoever heard of an American cheese worth eating? Canada's mousetrap was despised even by mice. Australia and New Zealand hadn't grown up; when they had they would perhaps learn to make something half as good as Stilton. The Irish, with some of the best dairyland in the world, were incapable of producing a cheese that wasn't as tasteless as a potato. Barbarians again! As for Germany, that demonstrated her lack of civilization so violently every generation – have you ever heard tell, demanded the Colonel, of a self-respecting German cheese?

So perhaps his quaint theory had a grain of sense in it. His yardstick for the measurement of civilization might be an odd one, but at any rate it was not so absurd as the current American standard, which judges a whole people by the modernity of their plumbing.

After lunch we would set out again over the stubbles that lay golden in the afternoon sun. We never made a great bag on these occasions, for we walked leisurely and as the Colonel grew old he became more and more inclined to pause in a gateway for a chat and a cigarette. He'd turn out his shooting-bag and demonstrate how one could infallibly tell a young partridge from an old one ('Bend back the upper mandible of its beak to see whether it's soft or hard'). Or he'd admire a 'red-legged un' he'd shot, a French partridge which he always called a Froggie. Or he'd ask us about an old song he'd heard, the Twelve Days of Christmas, which has the refrain 'And a partridge in a pear-tree'. Now who the devil, said he, ever saw a partridge sitting in a pear-tree, – or indeed in any sort of tree whatever? 'I bet it was a little owl; or maybe it was a missel-thrush puffed-out on a cold day.' None of us could explain that line; and to this day I can't make even a guess about the meaning of 'a partridge in a pear-tree'.

When the cigarettes were finished we moved on, across the stubbles that darkened as the sun declined. The brown coveys rose and scattered; the guns banged; the dogs wove to and fro in front of us whenever the line stood still. And when at tea-time we came to the last stubble and drove it in towards the farmhouse the sun was sinking low behind us and our long shadows went before, we were giants. With seven-league boots I seemed to stride down the hill. The Colonel, with his gun over his shoulder, was a Long Man with his club upraised, and we came down the last steep slope to the huddled byres.

Come Rain, Come Shine

Walking through High Beech Wood as the leaves fall, I observe some mummified bundles of feather and fur hanging from the hazel-twigs at the place where three rides meet: two crows like black and midnight hags, a skeleton jay with its blue cheek-feathers still incongruously sticking to its bare skull, a couple of weasels, an attenuated stoat, some little owls and a hawk whose proud head and aquiline beak like some ancient Roman's seem to scorn the very blowflies that buzz about it.

By these gruesome tokens, to which now and then he adds a new victim, Old Henry demonstrates that he is still the petty lord and tyrant over all that runs or flies in High Beech Wood. This old keeper is like a ghost from the past, and his world is as dead as his victims on the gibbet; the Squire who was his master is buried in the churchyard and the Squire's son who would have inherited High Beech is buried by the drifting sands of Libya, and the shooting is now owned by a syndicate from the city. They took over Henry with the shoot, mainly because he occupied the gamekeeper's cottage and could not lawfully be turned out; so although he is over eighty, he still walks the woodland paths he walked in his vigorous youth, still carries his old hammer-gun under his arm (though he rarely shoots anything with it), still sets his snares and gins in the runs which he knows as well as a townsman knows the streets of his own town.

His ears are still sharp enough to hear the fox's bark or the jay's warning screech or the twig cracked by a poacher's boot a hundred yards away; his eyes, bleared and misty with the years, can still spot the hovering hawk or the tell-tale empty cartridge-case in the ride or the broken bracken-frond where an intruder has passed by. Out of long habit he still wages war against his lifetime's foes – magpie and jay, hawk and owl, stoat, weasel, fox and half-wild cat, and those two-legged varmints, as he calls them, who sneak through the wood with their lurcher dogs on Saturday afternoons and Sundays. But there are few real poachers nowadays, and I think Old Henry secretly misses them. 'Bless you, in the days before the war' (he means the 1914 war, of course) 'they used to make a business of it, working in gangs, half a dozen of the varmints banded together.' From time to time, he will tell you, the gangs shot it out with the keepers in the dark wood at midnight, and once Old Henry tracked a man home to his cottage by the bloodtrail from his wounded leg! Foggy nights in winter were the most dangerous; for then the poachers brought their guns into the wood to shoot roosting pheasants, hoping the sound would be mistaken for the fog-signals on the nearby railway line. Those were the days! 'Why, master, I minds how in my dad's time, when he keepered here for Squire's father, they used to set *man-traps* at the edge of the wood; and Dad used to tell us how he once heard a varmint squealing in one, just as a trapped rabbit squeals. . . .'

One of the things that mark out Henry as an anachronism is his tremendous sense of the sanctity of private property. It always strikes me as a little strange that he who has never owned any land himself – who indeed has never owned anything save a hammer-gun, a few pounds' worth of furniture, half a dozen pullets and a fat pig – should guard so jealously the rights of his masters, who probably care very little about those rights anyhow. Picnickers at holiday-seasons, bluebell-pickers, even lovers playing their age-old games among the bracken, always stir Henry into a furious rage and he yells at them: 'Don't you know this is private property? Didn't you see the notice-board? Don't you know you're trespassing?' Then perhaps some pert wench – even girls seem to know the law nowadays – pipes up with 'Trespassers *can't* be prosecuted – said so on the wireless – so there!' and Old Henry, who has no book-learning, shuffles away discomfited. The law was different, surely, in the old Squire's day!

On the first shooting day he puts on his best pair of breeches, as he has done every October for sixty years – before that he didn't possess a best pair – and goes down to the main road to meet the guns. He touches his cap to the syndicate men just as he used to touch it to the Squire and the parson and their Lordships and the young gentlemen on leave from the Indian Army; but he no longer knows their names, nor, it seems, do they often remember his, for there are too many names to remember if you live in London-town. He leads them down to the first drive and shows them to their places, each marked with a piece of folded newspaper in a cleft stick; then he goes off to take charge of the beaters, who seem much more tiresome and unruly than beaters used to be – the boys sometimes cheek him, even the older men no longer treat him with the respect due to a Head Keeper; – alas, there are no underkeepers now! However, he keeps the rag-tag-and-bobtail lot in line somehow, keeps them tapping on the trees and shouting 'Yi-yi-yi' and because he's known the wood ever since he could walk he drives the pheasants straight and high and never fails to show the guns a good day's sport. When it is over he bundles up the birds and counts them and hands them out to the guests, touching his cap as he does so, just the same as in the Squire's day. But then it used to be:

'A cock and a hen each for the young gentlemen, Henry; and a brace of cocks for the vicar; and don't forget to take a brace each to all the tenants and to send three brace down to the cottage hospital.'

Somehow it's different now. The head of the syndicate, counting up the bag, turns to his friends and says 'Not bad. That's sixty-two at two pounds a brace!' – and there are none for the farmers and none for the hospital, for the way to run a week-end shoot, thinks the head of the syndicate, is to have your sport *and* show a bit of profit at the end of the season!

Henry takes his tip and touches his cap and hobbles back through the dusky wood collecting up the cleft marker-sticks on his way: a shadow among the shadows, a relic of the past.

One day as I walked along the ride I found by chance a tightly-folded wad of newspaper that had somehow survived the weathers in the hollow of an old tree. It was one of those bits of paper which Henry wedges into the cleft sticks; I unfolded it, and was astonished to find myself reading a report of the Coronation of King George the Fifth! They had better paper then, and better printing-ink, I dare say; and the old Squire, apparently, used nothing less substantial than copies of *The Times* to mark the positions of his guns. I walked on, and when I encountered Henry wandering round the woodside with his spaniel (which is almost as stiff in its joints as he is) I told him what I had found.

'1911?' he repeated. I don't know how much or how little the date meant to him, but it carried him back into the past. '1911? Ah, those were the days . . . Old Squire used to put down two thousand pheasants then . . . never shot less than two hundred brace on the opening day. We used to drive 'em over the valley down there. Squire said he liked to have 'em looking no bigger'n starlings. There was a greenhouse on t'other side of the valley and 'twas Squire's dearest wish to drop a bird on it and smash the glass. 'A fiver for you, Henry,' he used to say, 'if you can put a bird over me so high that he falls slap in the middle of that greenhouse!' And one day Squire did it. Pleased as punch, he was, couldn't have been more pleased if he'd come into a fortune. I had my fiver and it cost him another pound to mend the greenhouse glass. But, bless you, sovereigns was nothing to the gentry in those days. They'd have a ten pound sweep on who shot the first woodcock; and the winner would pick up a hundred or two. We keepers used to like that; it meant an extra tip for us if the gent who won was open-fisted.'

Wages were low then – Henry thought himself lucky to get fifty pounds a year and a decent cottage – but tips were frequent and generous. Nobody gave less than a fiver if the bag amounted to more than a hundred brace; or if they did they were not invited again! One guest, Henry remembers, was so remarkably mean that he slipped away without tipping at all; but it was the keeper's duty to clean and pack up the guns and Henry conveniently forgot to put them on the train. In due course the mean man wrote to his host, asking for the return of his pair of Purdeys, and the Squire who well understood the situation, wrote back regretting the delay, adding a pointed PS.:

'I never interfere with my keepers. *Perhaps you will get in touch with Henry?*'

A five-pound note arrived by return, and Henry sent off the guns with his humble apologies.

So Henry babbled on, as old men do, until a jay's screech called him back from the past suddenly and he picked up his gun, which must be older than himself, and touched his cap, and hobbled off into the wood. 'Well, I must be getting on with it . . . must chivvy up they troublesome jays.' A little later I heard a shot; and so I dare say the hawk and the owl, the weasels and the draggled crows, have new company on the gallows. There they swing from the hazel-twigs, dancing their dance of death whenever the wind blows, clicketty-clack when skeleton meets skeleton, old dry bones jigging together. And now the jay swings with them, and the flies buzz about it, and if you happen to pass downwind of the gallows-tree you will catch a whiff that used to identify the place to all who went by it, a mouldering whiff that belongs like Henry to the dead past.

Come Rain, Come Shine

HUNTING

Hunting is the noblest exercise
Makes men laborious, active, wise,
Brings health, and doth the spirits delight.
It helps the hearing and the sight . . .

                Ben Jonson

I think that John was always fascinated by the extraordinary and 'Squire Mytton' definitely came within that category. Before the war a new biography of Mytton was written by Mr Richard Darwall and John materially assisted the author by what the latter described as 'suggestions which were tactful as well as helpful'.

In 1935 Messrs. J.M. Dent & Sons Ltd published a book which had taken John three years to write when in his late twenties. This was entitled *Country Men* and contained several pages on Mytton, whose exceedingly strange life John had studied in some detail.

Some wintry pictures hung appropriately upon the walls of the Swan bar in the days when the Colonel used to come in hoar and half-frozen after standing knee-deep in flood-water waiting for duck. They represented the exploits of John Mytton, and the Colonel never tired of them, for he had a fellow-feeling for one who would stalk wild duck across a frozen lake by moonlight, clad only in his night-shirt; it was the kind of thing he might have done himself in his young days. He particularly liked the picture of Mytton setting fire to his night-shirt 'to frighten his damned hiccups away'; and of course he loved the very lively Alken drawing of Mytton riding into his dining-room upon the back of a bear, a feat which he undertook in order to frighten the tame clergyman who was a supernumerary of his large household, holding a position in the establishment somewhat similar to that of the tame bear. The Colonel, who disliked parsons on principle, much as Cobbett did, used to chuckle over this picture, rejoicing in the cleric's discomfiture. 'Look at the dam' feller, climbing up on the table!'

Then there was the print which showed the famous gig episode. Mytton was tearing along a country lane with a timid passenger who protested at the pace.

'Was you ever much hurt, then, by being upset in a gig?' asked Squire Mytton.

'No, thank God,' answered the passenger, 'for I never was upset in one.'

'What?' cried Mytton. 'Never upset in a gig? What a damned slow fellow you must have been all your life!' – and with that he ran the near wheel up the bank and over they went, horse, gig and all. The damned slow fellow was not seriously hurt, and subsequently with astonishing fortitude he married Mytton's daughter. If he hoped for an inheritance, he was unlucky; for Mytton succeeded in getting rid of half a million pounds in fifteen years, which took a bit of doing in those days if one's extravagances were of the more or less normal kind, e.g. drink, horses, gambling and girls. Unfortunately Mytton added some extraordinary prodigalities of his own. He had a curious objection to paper money, and to demonstrate his contempt for it he would sometimes *eat* a five pound note laid upon a piece of bread and butter. Or he would throw away wads of £100 or so as he walked round his estate; or he would let a thousand or two blow out of his coach on a windy night as he came spanking home from the races.

He decided to stand for Parliament, and rode through Shrewsbury, his chosen constituency, handing out £10 notes to anybody who held forth a hand. The election cost him £10,000 and he duly went to Westminster. He spent exactly half an hour in the House of Commons, which he decided was stuffy and dull. So he came home, and resumed his fox-hunting. He never went to the House again.

Instead he took to drinking six bottles of port a day, for which in his later years he substituted six bottles of brandy. His end was sad and no doubt satisfactory to the moralists; for he whose days had been spent in the pursuit of almost every conceivably huntable creature was now himself hunted by his creditors up and down the length and breadth of England. He escaped for a time to Calais ('with a couple of bum-baillies hard on his brush'); and it was while he was there, being troubled one night by the hiccups, that he set his night-shirt on fire. He was severely burned, but he bore the pain with stoical courage, writing from what he truly believed to be his death-bed self-mocking notes to his friends, – in which, incidentally, he correctly quoted Horace, Sophocles and the Bible in Greek! He must have had a remarkable memory, for I doubt if he had ever read a book since his schooldays.

When at last urgent business, or nostalgia, or merely whim brought him back to England his creditors gathered about him once more. He was arrested and imprisoned at the King's Bench in London; and there he died, in *delirium tremens*, at the age of 38.

He was crazy, useless, profligate – I give you all that; yet his galloping career surely has its moments of wild splendour. 'Light come, light go' is the title of Alken's picture of the bank notes blowing out of the coach. It is a moonlight night, and windy, with ragged clouds chasing each other across the moon. The four horses, as usual, are at full gallop.

The money streams out behind the coach like the paper tail of a boy's kite; and within sits Mytton uncaring. There are people who believe money to be something sacred; and the print must shock those people profoundly. Bank Managers, I am sure, would like to put it upon an *Index Expurgatorius*. But for my part I like a man who throws money away better than one who counts it three times before he goes to bed; and so I have a soft spot in my heart for the memory of poor Jack Mytton.

I've a soft spot too – who hasn't? – for Alken's delightful prints. Most of all I like his aquatints of gentlemen out shooting in top-hats, cutaway coats and (one would think) unsuitable trousers, pursuing ducks, pheasants and hares in bright and snowy weather. The artist always makes his one concession to the dramatic moment and to his subject's self-esteem; for each muzzle-loader that has been fired there is at least one mallard or cock-pheasant in a flurry of feathers tumbling out of the sky. Likewise in the fishing-prints the angler is always attended by a dutiful keeper carrying the net, the creel and the inevitable brace of trout or pike; for there were no blank days in that beautiful aquatinted world of Alken.

You will notice too that in the hunting-pictures of the period the running hounds are always so tightly packed that, as foxhunters say in their pleasant hyperbole, 'You could cover them with a handkerchief'. And this, I suppose, was the artist's necessary compliment to the M.F.H. who had commissioned the painting and whose hounds in real life perhaps straggled over half his hunting-country and ran riot chasing rabbits, hares and old maids' tabbies. Perhaps the plenitude of falls which are shown in these pictures was a kind of compliment too, suggesting what devil-may-care fellows the riders were. At any rate the artist was always at pains to show some examples of what was called 'Grief'. Somebody had to fall, and generally to smash the top of a five-barred gate in the course of doing so.

The red fox streaking across the field, the eager hounds at his brush, and of course the horses, are always shown with their forelegs stretched out forward, their hindlegs stretched out behind, and the belly close to the ground. No living creature gallops like this; and it has been ingenuously suggested that until the invention of railway-trains, from which fast-moving passengers could observe the movements of fast-moving creatures running parallel with themselves, people really believed that horses galloped in such a fashion. This of course is sheer nonsense; so is the idea that photography suddenly demonstrated to man something which his own eye had always been too slow to perceive. In fact, the human eye acts more quickly than did the best Victorian cameras; and many painters drew horses correctly – that is to say, as *we* see them – hundreds of years ago. It was, I think, simply a convention in the 18th and early 19th century to paint horses *ventre à terre*: it seemed to make them move faster. And so we see a coach with every one of its team stretched out in this unnatural way going like billy-o from London to Birmingham. And we see the Midnight Steeplechasers in that ubiquitous set of prints, streaking through the night on steeds that would surely have split themselves if they had really galloped so.

The first midnight steeplechase took place near Ipswich. The riders were some of the officers of a cavalry regiment quartered there; the prints show them with blue trousers bearing a yellow stripe. They wore, by agreement, night-shirts and night-caps; and the prints capture most perfectly the ghostly moonlight pallor shining on the night-caps as the horsemen tore across country in that crazy race, slap across country from the barracks to some church that had a visible spire. Six finished; and in the last print we see them galloping down the village street, singing 'The Lads of the Village', hollering and whooping, with all the inhabitants, night-shirted and holding candles, leaning out of their windows and cheering the winner. Would they cheer nowadays? They would probably complain to the police, or write to the papers about the ill-behaviour of the Idle Rich disturbing the well-deserved slumbers of the Workers.

The Swan was an old coaching house; and pride of place among the pictures in the bar was given to a print which showed the inn as it had been in 1830 – a winter day as usual, for the artists in those days were much addicted to snowy scenes – steam rising in clouds from the backs of the horses and coming from their nostrils in jets as from the funnels of the Puffing-Billies that were so soon to replace them. The mail coach had just arrived from London, having taken very little longer over the journey that British Railways take to-day. I can imagine it coming full canter up Elmbury High Street, horseshoes sparking on the cobbles, root-toot-toot on the horn, everybody rushing out of the Swan yard to meet it. I love the air of *busyness* about these old coaching pictures. Things may have been a trifle quiet at the inn betweenwhiles, but when the Mail comes in, what a buzz, what a hum, what a running to and fro of neat little waitresses and stable boys and grooms! The sweating horses are taken out of the shafts, led to the stables, brushed down and the worst of the mud washed off their fetlocks while they are being watered . . . Crushed oats poured out into the mangers, hay stuffed in the racks, a linseed mash mixed in a bucket if the horses are tired and the night is cold! And meanwhile the fresh horses are harnessed up, restive, well-corned, glossy as cob-nuts; the ostlers bustle about – hostlers as they were then correctly called – green-aproned, shirt-sleeved, tightly-breeked; and the postboys carry out foaming tankards in which the ale or porter is always so much frothier than we see it today. The whole sense of the picture is one of warm welcome; what fun, you think, it must have been to arrive at an inn after a long cold journey in 1830. But alas, nowadays the chances are that you will be frigidly received by a sour-faced thin-lipped female more suitable for employment in a Food Office during the strictest period of rationing, she whom they call the Receptionist, though I often think she would be better named a Rejectionist as she snaps out 'Have you booked?', obviously hoping you haven't so that she may have the extreme pleasure of telling you the hotel is full.

Come Rain, Come Shine

John wrote a weekly column for the *Birmingham Mail* for no less than eighteen years, and I do not think that he ever missed a single issue; indeed, he produced his customary article the week before his death. Phil Drabble (who most kindly wrote the Foreword to this anthology) took over the column which he is still writing today, twenty years later!

I have been reading about some of the crazy foxhunting squires in the days of the Regency. Shropshire was the home of many of them; even today I sense a wild spirit about its lovely Border countryside. There was John Mytton, for instance, the Squire of Halston, who got rid of half a million pounds in fifteen years. If he paid a call on you he was likely to ride his one-eyed hunter Baronet up the steps and through the front door, along the corridor and into the sitting-room. And there they'd settle down, horse and man on opposite sides of your hearth, drinking mulled port (which Baronet seems to have enjoyed as much as his master) until the small hours.

John Mytton, being presented by his wife with a son and heir, had it christened Euphrates, after a racehorse he owned. The child died as it happened, in infancy, so didn't have to bear his ridiculous Christian name among the young bullies at Eton . . .

There was a fellow called Boycott, likewise a Salopian, who also returned from foxhunting to find an addition to his family. But this was a girl. After dinner he suggested that his guests should draw lots to decide who should name the child. A drunken fellow who won the draw decided that 'Foxhunter Moll' would be suitable; and since a drunken parson was also present she was christened then and there. Foxhunter Moll Boycott became a famous horsewoman, though her husband observed of her, rather sadly one feels, that she was 'more of a good fellow than a wife'.

Another Shropshire foxhuntress was called Phoebe Higgs. She was handsome and utterly reckless – 'the most daring horsewoman that ever rode to hounds'. She became the mistress of Squire George Forester of the village of Willey, who already had several mistresses, all chosen for their horsemanship as well as for their other attributes. Apparently they all lived at Willey Hall at the same time: and this led to bickering, to some extent. One day Phoebe discovered that one of the other ladies was receiving a larger allowance than herself. Like Frankie in the ballad she provided herself with a pistol. She pointed it at Squire Forester and demanded a bigger allowance than her rival. She got it.

Squire Mytton, to the dismay of his friends and servants, populated Halston Hall with wild animals, including a monkey (which he mounted on a hunter and took out with the hounds) and a bear (which he himself rode late at night, to the alarm of his guests, until one evening it turned and bit him in the leg). A bear in those days was frequently to be found in a great Squire's establishment – which included all manner of supernumeraries, ranging from a pet prize-fighter and a personal parson to a peacock.

Birmingham Mail, 26 November 1965

THE SQUIRE

Just opposite the Nurse's cottage are the 'big gates' of Downend Drive. It is told of the Squire's grandfather, who was a very impatient man, that on an occasion when he came back late from hunting he failed to make his lodge-keeper hear him, in spite of his angry shouting, and rather than dismount he put his famous old horse Greatheart at the gates full-gallop, though they were made of wrought iron and are more than six feet high. He survived the fall, as he survived a hundred others, only to achieve the distinction four years later of being nearly the first man in England to be run over by a motor-car.

The present Squire is another of the same type: a hard-riding, angry, blustering, swearing man, rather like William the Conqueror. He has broken so many bones, including his pelvis, that he is no longer able to grip the saddle with his knees: but he still hunts his own hounds, although he cannot jump, and by means of his intimate knowledge of the country and his skill at gates he succeeds in keeping up with them even when the whips are left behind. A talkative stranger went up to him at a meet last season and said:

'That's a good-lookin' horse you've got, Master. Will he jump?'

'I'll shoot the b— if he does,' said the Squire.

Yet however good the scent, however swift and faultless the hounds, however straight-running the fox, the Squire always manages somehow or other to be there when his pack kills or marks to ground. He knows every gate and gap, every short cut, every ride through the woods. This knowledge saves him many miles of galloping in every run; and it is coupled with a fierce and angry determination to be first, a sort of perpetual boiling rage which drives him *through* all the obstacles which other people go over or round. When hounds are running the Squire will drawn rein for neither man, woman, nor child. He will gallop hell-for-leather along the village street, crash through the fence into your garden and curse you most horribly if he finds he can't get out at the other end. Not the Devil himself – and certainly not an angel with a flaming sword – could stop him when he is careering in this fashion after his hounds.

It is strange that he, who loves hunting better than anything else in the world, should always appear to be in a furious temper when he is on a horse. He is Masefield's 'old bear in a scarlet pelt' to the life. He often terrifies non-hunting strangers by galloping threateningly towards them and bawling *'Have You seen My Fox?* Haven't you got a tongue in your head, damn and blast you?' And he is equally rude to any of the members of the Hunt who happen to get in his way or who otherwise annoy him. One morning in the cubbing season a lady held up her hand to stop him as he came splashing down a muddy ride and when he yelled 'What the devil's the matter?' she said;

'Your fox has only just crossed, Master.'

'Did you see him?'

'No, I can smell him. I've got a very sharp nose.'

'Better breed hounds from you,' he shouted, as he spurred his horse and galloped past her.

You might easily conclude that the Squire was a perfectly insufferable person, a bully and a tyrant dreaded and hated by everybody. Yet the truth is that he is loved, and the people who love him best are those who have most reason to fear him – his tenants, his servants, the labourers on his estate. This strikes one as all the more surprising since the Squire of a neighbouring village, who possesses all the virtues of good manners which our Squire lacks, is mistrusted and disliked by every man and woman on his estate. Here, then, is a paradox. Our Squire is a noisy, swearing, terrifying fellow who'll damn your eyes for tuppence: the neighbouring Squire is a soft-spoken, diffident man who addresses all his farmers as 'Mister' So-and-so and 'wouldn't say boo to a goose'. How shall we explain it?

The reason, I think, is partly that country people fear most the thing they do not understand. Our Squire is easy to understand: his father and his grandfather lived here before him, and in a sense he is one of us. The neighbouring Squire is comparatively a stranger even to his own tenants. He is a director of many big companies and spends half his time in London. We know hardly anything of his life, his family, his pleasures, his opinions. We don't know what he does with the money we pay him in rent, nor how he gets the money to pay us for our labour.

But the life of our own Squire is an open book to us. He uses his rents to buy horses and hounds and pedigree Hereford cattle, to keep his farm buildings in repair, to plant trees. Better the devil we know than the devil we don't! Besides, if a tenant farmer has a bad year, and he goes to Squire on audit-day and tells him frankly, 'I can't afford to pay you,' Squire will say:

'All right, damn you, pay me when you can.'

But if a tenant goes to the neighbouring Squire with a similar request, he receives the polite answer;

'Er—well—Mr So-and-so—of course you realize this is a very serious matter which I must discuss with my Agent.'

A few weeks later, if the rent isn't paid, the farmer gets his notice to quit.

Better by far the devil you know! Our countrymen are the Secret People of G. K. Chesterton's poem, 'the people of England, that never has spoken yet'. They fear their new masters far more than they feared the old ones. For the country squires, for the most part, were at any rate honest: they loved the land and they held it as a trust, to be administered fairly and well. The new financiers have given little proof of their honesty: they do not belong to the country and they regard the land as a commodity to be bought and sold for profit like jute or coal or corn. We mistrust their motives and we fear their cleverness. Well may the Secret People say:

We only know that the last sad squires ride slowly towards the sea
And a new people takes the land; and still it is not we.

They have given us into the hands of the new unhappy lords,
Lords without anger or honour, who dare not carry their swords.
They fight by shuffling papers; they have bright dead alien eyes;
They look at our labour and laughter as a tired man looks at flies.
And the load of their loveless pity is worse than the ancient wrongs,
Their doors are shut in the evening; and they know no songs.

The Countryman's England

The Meet was handy, so instead of taking the horse-box they rode there together, she on Nightshade, he on Trumpeter, which she had persuaded Janet to lend him. Most of the day was spent in the big coverts. They cantered up and down the muddy rides, got splashed and spattered all over, stood now and then at the crossings listening to the occasional yelping and to the high-pitched voice of General Bouverie swearing alliteratively. The hard-riding ones grumbled at a hunting day wasted, but Susan enjoyed being with Stephen and showing him the woods she knew so well. Their talk ranged from Trollope to

Teddy-boys and from Mozart to men on Mars. They spotted a buzzard circling like a sailplane three hundred feet above them, saw three foxes, a weasel, a stoat and a badger, which looked cross and sleepy as if he had just been woken up by the hounds. And standing by a hazel-brake at the edge of the wood they watched a big flock of long-tailed tits, a score of them at least, flitting from twig to twig, blown along by the big wind which turned their tails inside out like ladies' parasols in a gale. They were like little trapeze artists upon the swaying hazel-wands doing extraordinary acrobatics, more often upside-down than right-side up: and during a brief blink of sunlight they looked so pretty, in their brown-and-white-and-rosy plumage, that Susan turned to Stephen in sheer delight, and saw her pleasure reflected in his eyes.

'This is surely the nicest sort of foxhunting,' he said.

Then suddenly out of the dark wood, which up to that moment had been as quiet as the grave, came an astonishing extempore clamour: a kind of thunderclap of hounds' voices, all speaking together. The cries fused into a single yell. The fox must have jumped up right in front of the pack; anxious in case she might head it back into the wood, Susan edged Nightshade close up to the hazels and beckoned Stephen to her side. Knee to knee they waited there; the horses quivered and flexed their ears. Stephen said quietly:

'Which way do you think he'll go?'

'Over the brook by those willows, then straight for the Park!'

'Sukie, I'm scared stiff!' he said.

The admission took her by surprise; he had such an air of insouciance always.

'I wouldn't have thought you'd have been scared of things.'

'I am though! Making a speech in the House. Climbing mountains.'

'But you love them, don't you?'

'Love them; but frightened all the same.'

'What about the war?' she whispered.

'By turns bored and terrified.'

'What were you in?'

'Commandos.'

Just then the hounds came crashing through the hazels. The fox must have run up the ditch at the edge of the covert; at any rate Susan didn't catch a glimpse of it. She reined in Nightshade to let the screaming pack go by.

'Why *them,* if you were terrified?' she asked Stephen over her shoulder; and there was just time to hear his answer.

'If you were Jewish as well as British you had one *extra* reason for wanting to get at the bloody Huns.'

Then they were off. The hounds were well out in the field now, and streaking towards the willows. The huntsman was with them, and General Bouverie on an enormous horse had come crashing out of the hazels like an elephant bashing its way through bamboos. Susan rode side by side with Stephen to the brook; it was only a little one, and both horses took it in their stride. The hounds were screaming mad and their cry drove Susan mad, she yelled to Stephen 'Listen to them, oh, listen!' but the wind blew away the words when they were scarcely past her lips. Stephen had noticed that the pack was beginning to swing left-handed, and now without a glance at Susan he turned hard left in quick anticipation and galloped for the fence in the corner against the wood. Susan knew that post-and-rails. It was as tall and solid as if the farmer had wanted to confine kangaroos instead of Hereford cattle. Left to herself she would have gone for the gate at the opposite corner, trusting to her good start to reach it and get through it before the rest of the field caused a hold-up there. But Stephen was pounding hard for the post-and-rails, so she accepted the challenge – wouldn't Nightshade jump the course at Aintree with her legs tied together? (For a fraction of a second she remembered Stow Fair. She saw Tony bargaining with the dealer in the bright sun. The memory warmed her whole spirit; then the wind seemed to blow it away.)

Stephen was over the post-and-rails. Here goes: she was over too. She had the impression that there had been a lot of daylight between Stephen's breeches and the saddle. He hadn't hunted since before the war, but Trumpeter was an arm-chair of a horse, unlikely to peck or stumble. Stephen, still with a short cut in mind, now led the the way through a clump of scattered trees which straggled out from the edge of the wood. He shouted to her over his shoulder, 'Absalom my son, my son – look out!' and tucked his head into Trumpeter's neck as he tore between the oak boughs. Then they were clear of the wood altogether, and galloping down the long slope with a good view of the pack racing up the hillside opposite them. Susan could see a flock of sheep forming themselves into a kind of defensive phalanx, and what she took to be a collie-dog about thirty yards from the sheep. Then she realised it was the fox, only a field in front of the pack. He was going straight for the Park, as she had thought he would.

The next hedge was a hell of a thing, mixed blackthorn and hawthorn, which looked even taller than it was because it hadn't been properly trimmed at the top. It was black and solid and there was a big drop on the far side; and the approach to it was downhill all the way. It was one of those obstacles where you have to 'throw your heart over first and follow it as best you can'. Stephen had already thrown his. He'd decided the place where he was going to jump and had aimed Trumpeter at it. Susan prayed that he would guess about the drop on the other side, and she was angry with him for risking his neck, and risking Trumpeter, just to show off in front of her, or perhaps to try to prove that he wasn't really as old as it said in *Who's Who*. (Born 1909; so he was forty-two.)

She took her eyes off him, while she looked after herself and Nightshade. Going faster than Susan liked, the mare rose like a bird and simply flew the tall hedge. Susan lay right back and pretended she was riding in the National. Nightshade landed neatly, collected herself, and was off up the opposite hill. Susan out of the corner of her eye saw Trumpeter going well; but now with a long grass field before her, and Nightshade's splendid stride lengthening, she easily caught up with Stephen and decided she'd have no more nonsense: 'Follow me, I know every inch from here; he's making for Ferdinando's Oak.' It was a good half-mile, all uphill, and Susan doubted whether the fox would make it; but the pack had checked when he ran among the sheep, and he reached the big badgers' earth with minutes to spare. When Susan got there the hounds were milling round the tree, General Bouverie was swearing Blast and bloody shipwreck because the earth hadn't been stopped, and there was nobody except the huntsman within two hundred yards.

'Here comes your perishing politician,' the General shouted at her. 'I thought he was going to break his bloody neck.' He hated all politicians, irrespective of party, because they were responsible for the Income Tax. Susan had left Stephen behind when they were over the last fence before the Park. He cantered up to her now with Trumpeter in a foaming lather; the old horse had a look in his eye which seemed to be asking Susan what kind of a devil she had put upon his back. As for Stephen, he'd smeared some blood from a thorn scratch all over his nose, and looking a bit clownish he gave Susan a most endearing grin, composed of guilt, mischief, relief that he was alive and unhurt, and a sort of boyish conceit which he ought to have grown out of long ago – so that she forgave him for showing off and liked him even better than she had done before.

Now the terrier man arrived in a Land-Rover which he'd driven round by Elmbury Back Lane. General Bouverie, with oaths, shouted for spades and a mattock. The terriers whimpered on their leash. The First Whip and the Huntsman gathered up the pack and took it away from the tree, which dwarfed the men and the horses standing beneath its gaunt and wintry boughs.

Susan wondered if Ferdinando's Owl was there, his feathers fluffed out, his head turned right round to see what was going on, his great eyes wide open in annoyance at the clamour that had broken into his sleep. Was there a red squirrel there too? she wondered – and hoped it wouldn't jump down in panic, for the hounds were in a mood to tear to pieces any furry thing. Were the badgers at home, grunting at the fox which had sought refuge in their sett? Were the bats waking up in the hollow trunk, their wings crackling like old parchment?

From where she was, on the slope below the tree, she got a fine view of it against the sky, in which ragged dove-grey windy clouds raced each other across a patch of wan cold starling's-egg blue. The pattern of the bare boughs was familiar; she'd been brought up with the pattern, she would have known straight away if anything was different, if one of the boughs had carried away in a gale. The tree was part of her background. She remembered the games with Rosemary, and climbing with Tony, and Rosemary only the other day in the foggy dusk confessing about her baby; and the owl and the bats and the squirrels, and the badgers which she'd once watched by moonlight with Tony at her side. It was a special tree, and she thought the fox ought to have sanctuary there, it wouldn't be proper to dig him out from among the ancient roots and chuck him clay-streaked and bedraggled to the still-whimpering hounds. So she rode up to General Bouverie, much more frightened than she had ever been during the run, and dared to say:

'Please, Master, do you mind if we leave him where he is?'

'Leave my fox?' roared the general, who always assumed that any fox he chased was his personal property. He goggled at her alarmingly, with hot eyes in a windscorched face; then, just as she was beginning to explain why Ferdinando's Oak was a kind of sanctuary (and was feeling rather a fool as she did so) he cut her short with another roar: 'Well, it's your blasted tree and your perishing Park. You'd have had his brush if we'd caught him, so if you want to save him for another day' – and a slow smile spread over his formidable face like a hint of spring upon a winter land. He clambered on to his huge horse and yelled and swore at his Huntsman and his Whips and his hounds, and the oaths ringing in their ears meant no more to any of them than the crow's cawing, or the jackdaws' raucous chatter as they flew overhead towards their roosts in Elmbury Abbey tower.

Hounds and horsemen trotted off down the long slope. The wind sighed in Ferdinando's branches. Somewhere in the dark, down among the gnarled roots, lay the panting fox, his muddy sides heaving. Susan was pleased by the thought of him lying so cosy there, and she smiled happily at Stephen as they rode on together up the hill towards the Manor, and heard far below them the long thin quavering day's-end blast of the horn.

* * *

They ran hard, as Janet had said they would – six miles as the fox went, four and a bit as the crows flew, to a furzy waste on the very edge of the General's hunting-country, called Brockeridge. The fox took refuge there in a sort of catacombs of badger-earths; and because it was a rocky place, that had once been a quarry, the General decided not to try to dig him out.

Meanwhile the rain had stopped, the sky had cleared, and the wind which had been backing steadily all morning swung right round and blew hard from the opposite direction; so that a second fox, which they found in some scrub that lay close to the common, ran the opposite way to his predecessor – towards Doddington instead of away from it. He was what the old hunting journalists would have called a straight-necked 'un, and he went as hard as he could across the flat river meadows towards the sanctuary of the distant woodland. The meadows were huge, the fences were tall, well-made ones, it was very like riding in a race. Susan as she galloped felt her kinship with those Regency bucks, her ancestors, their wild spirits like a high wind blowing through hers! She told herself exultantly that she'd rather be doing this, at this particular moment, than anything else she could think of in the world; and over a fence that had a wide ditch on the near side of it she made the firm decision, between take-off and landing, that she would enter her lovely Nightshade in the Ladies' Race at the Point-to-Point next March.

A mile short of Doddington, her mother had to pull up; Trumpeter had burst a little vessel in his nose, not a very serious matter in itself, but of course the blood pumped out of it when he was galloping. It mixed with foam from his mouth and blew over Janet so that when Susan last saw her she looked like the sort of blood-boltered monster which the League Against Cruel Sports doubtless imagined a hunting woman to be.

The clamorous pack ran on. Over the main road – Susan jumped on to it and off it, and got a wave from a lorry driver who'd pulled up to let the hounds go by. Into the trees where dusk was falling, full tilt along the leaf-strewn rides, out into the light again and over the Park, and so to Seven Men's Tump, where the elms stood black and gaunt against a sky that faded from primrose to a starling's-egg blue. They killed just short of the Tump, and Susan was one of a dozen or so who saw the stretched-out pack, ghost-hounds in the twilight, close up together suddenly and rearrange themselves into a swirling mêlée on the slope of the hill.

The Waters under the Earth

Walking through those woods, it occurred to Mr Wigglesworth – how much longer would men be able to hunt the red fox? Ten years, twenty, twenty-five? And how would the end come – by economic necessity, the spread of towns, the increase of barbed wire, the multiplication of small enclosures of land? Or by the legislation of a raving horde of sentimentalists, who thought it finer (since obviously foxes must be killed) to chance a snatched shot at the marauder in the half-light, and let him die of a festering gunshot wound, or to poison his grub, or to keep a vixen suffering agonies with her pad in a trap while her cubs starved, than to chase Reynard with the swift beautiful hounds and the stout-hearted horses with brave men astride them over a risky country?

But what did it matter how the end came? It was inevitable, as was the vanishing of all beautiful things.

'And if I'm alive then . . .?' thought Mr Wigglesworth. There would be only books left: books and a little thought, before the final blacking-out of consciousness. Mr Wigglesworth's revolution was near an end.

*   *   *

They had hunted their big dog otter, in twelve feet of water, from eleven o'clock in the morning, when Ralph had holloaed him over the falls, until five o'clock in the afternoon, when they pushed him down to the ford and killed him. Now the field had dispersed, some in motor-cars, some to the nearest station, some on foot. Ralph and Marjorie were among the latter – Ralph with his stiff horseman's walk and Marjorie with the easy unhurrying stride of perfect fitness. She was as hard as nails, yet graceful; beautiful with her bright cheeks and clear eyes, her slim figure, soft and delicately moulded, yet tough and taut as chisel-steel, her bare head shining in the sunlight. Her stockings, her short skirt for its last six inches, were dripping wet; the sleeves of her jumper were rolled up to the elbows.

Squelch! went Ralph's otter-hunting shoes, drilled through the bottom so that the water ran out of them. It was a good seven-mile walk back to Middlewick; they could have had a lift, but Marjorie, with her boundless energy, had insisted on footing it. 'It's such a lovely evening, Ralph!' He watched her with admiration. Thirty miles a day would knock most girls out.

It had been a wonderful hunt. Not, thought Ralph, not that you could compare otter-hunting with the chase of the fox, the glorious feeling of having a horse beneath you, the exhilaration of the jump, the swift racing pack, the red fellow streaking in front. . . . In otter-hunting Ralph could never quite rid himself of a sneaking pity for the quarry, with his sharp, sleek head and little unflinching eyes, and beautiful swift dive through the clear water. Ralph always felt that there was something a little bullying, something not altogether fair and square, about the chase of the brave, friendly otter. These spring days were not the time for hunting. . . .

On the other hand, you learned more about hounds in this sport than you did in years of fox- and stag- and harrier-hunting. The big, shaggy fellows, how he loved them! What a joy it was to see them feather along the bank – Dustman, Warrior, Pitiful, Pillager, lame Wickhamby; rough-coated Waterwitch, Masterful, Denis, David, all the rest of them. Ten couple of sterns fanning slowly, then faster, then faster, and none daring to speak to it; and then all those twenty dappled tails moving in unison, like a patch of slender, agitated flowers; and then the whimper that became a yell, a crash, a thunder. Music like wine, the most thrilling sound in the universe.

And the deep-throated bellow of Dexter, the old trusty hound, when finally he marked at the end of the long drag! The dark form shooting out of the willow-tree like a torpedo from a ship's side. The splash, widening ripples, bubbles leading upstream . . . And then Ralph would go mad, running knee-deep through the swift cold water, with the hounds crying in front.

Such jolly people came out with the Wye Valley, Ralph's own kind, the hard, friendly country-folk. A bare dozen, but a dozen of the best: men who had fought and steeplechased and travelled and hunted all their lives; men who lived quietly in big, rambling farmhouses, women who could walk thirty miles a day without showing it; girls who weren't above drinking a glass of beer with you in a country inn. They were a very select company. Sometimes there were visitors, men in the blue uniform and red caps of the Hawkstone or the Bucks; and often an inquisitive rabble of sightseers followed for a mile or two; but only that select dozen or so were with the hounds always. It was an esoteric circle whose mysteries were the names of hounds, recognized without error, and the ways of rivers and brooks and otters.

The music of the hounds, thought Ralph, made him mad and drunk with the sound of it; it led him down to the river as the Pied Piper led the rats at Hamelin. Dexter, Warrior, Dustman, Pillager; great voices belling deep down in a stream among the rocks; solitary tongues calling, threatening, yelling for blood; and then the crash of the whole pack of them in unison, which is like no other sound in the whole world. He could sympathize with that famous old huntsman who requested that when they buried him they should give three mighty view-holloas over his coffin; and if that failed to stir him, they could put him under the ground with untroubled minds. 'If the cry of hounds failed to wake me,' thought Ralph, 'then I should be dead indeed!'

Dixon's Cubs

A glimpse into the past. . . . In his Introduction to a modern edition of Nimrod's *Life of a Sportsman* (published by John Lehmann in 1948) John wrote of the Jeunesse Dorée of 150 years earlier with insight and a certain sympathy, admiring the courage of the Meltonians of the day, though by no means disregarding their faults. This was typical of John, who was usually willing to 'give the Devil his due' and slow to condemn others, even though possibly they deserved condemnation.

As I have written elsewhere in this anthology, he was always fascinated by the extraordinary, and the characters portrayed in Nimrod's little-known novel of 1832 included some strange (and perfectly authentic) individuals. The author (whose real name was Charles James Apperley) was the famous biographer of John Mytton, one of the greatest eccentrics of all time, for whom John admitted having a 'soft spot'.

C. J. Apperley was born at Plâs-gronow in Denbighshire in the year 1779 in circumstances which I am sure he would have described as tragic: he was born a gentleman, but without any money. Gentlemen of his time, especially if they were hunting gentlemen, were apt to believe that they had a prescriptive right to ten thousand a year; and poor young Apperley, who was following the hounds in a red coat at the age of twelve, quickly acquired a taste for the two most expensive pastimes of his day – foxhunting in Leicestershire, and coaching with a crack four-in-hand. Of course drinking was expensive too, when a wine-merchant's annual bill of £500 was regarded as moderate; and you could also get rid of your fortune quite quickly on the racecourse, in the gambling halls, and at the ringside, or by the simpler expedient of Squire Mytton, who thought so little of the new paper currency that he let his £5 notes blow about the Shropshire countryside or even put them between pieces of bread and ate them. In the hot Regency atmosphere the greatest estates often melted away like butter (Mytton, actually, got rid of half a million in fifteen years), for there were so many expensive things and people perpetually draining away at the Corinthian's purse: horses and grooms, hounds and huntsmen, pheasants and keepers, coaches and curricles, pointers and greyhounds, gamecocks and prizefighters, tailors and harness-makers, down to the tame parsons, tutors, bears and monkeys which formed as it were the supernumeraries of a gentleman's enormous establishment. Women, as it happened, contributed but little to the almost inevitable ruin of the Melton men, who hunted six days a week and went to church on Sundays, so had neither the time nor energy left to pursue them.

The unfortunate Mr Apperley, compelled to earn his own living at a time when there were few polite means of doing so, served for a short period in Ireland with Sir Watkin Wynn's Ancient British Light Dragoons. But soldiering was not to his taste so he resigned his commission and came home. Then he married a lady who had a little – but not enough – money, and he tried his hand at farming in a gentlemanly and unsuccessful way. Finally he was driven to the indignity of writing for his living, and his lively reminiscences of 'The Chace, the Road and the Turf' began to appear under the pseudonym of 'Nimrod' in what he slightingly called 'that mere Cockney concern', *The Sporting Magazine*. They met with such immediate success that *The Sporting Magazine* was able to put up its price, and before long bootpolish and breeches, a newspaper and a stage-coach, were all named after 'Nimrod'.

The world he wrote of – the happy-go-lucky, ten-thousand-a-year world – was never quite within his reach. He dwelt on the fringe of it and from time to time got a precarious foothold inside it as a nobleman's or rich squire's guest. But he was nevertheless its loving and faithful historian, and it may be that he wrote all the better because that world was never completely his own. Awe, admiration, even perhaps a tinge of envy, added zest to his writing as the appetite is sharpened by the contemplation of a forbidden feast. Francis Raby, the fortunate hero of *The Life of a Sportsman,* is poor Nimrod as he would have liked to have been, as he felt quite certain he would have been if only he had had his rights of ten thousand a year. Alas, his own circumstances when he wrote the book were sadly different from Francis Raby's. Melton Mowbray was left far behind, and he'd already been hunted to Calais by the usual 'two-couple of bumbaillies hard on his brush'. Melton must have seemed to him then as Eden did to Adam when he was cast out of it. He therefore gave himself over to those pipe-dreams which nowadays it is fashionable to call wishful thinking. Wishful thinking, however, has produced a lot of good books, and *The Life of a Sportsman* is no exception. Nimrod wrote well because he loved and longed; and it is irrelevant that the things he wrote about were, in our modern view, rather vain and trivial and worthless things. The story of Francis Raby will always be read by sportsmen because of its vivid and exciting descriptions of foxhunting in its heydey, and for the rest of us it remains an accurate, fascinating and by no means unimportant piece of social history.

Let us glance for a moment at this microcosmos of 150 years ago in which the imaginary Francis Raby was born and in which the wistful Nimrod longed to have his being. It is a very extraordinary little world, being full of contradictions: elegant 'refinement' goes side by side with beastly cruelty, hard riding with Augustan scholarship, elaborate polish with insensitive coarseness, and artificial manners with boisterous practical jokes. It is a world in which Francis Raby is brought up to hunt cats and bait badgers with his terriers at the age of ten, and yet discouraged from the 'cruel practice of angling with live worms'; a world in which young gentlemen who were the pink of courtesy in the saloon and the ballroom nevertheless found their greatest pleasure in the company of coachmen, prizefighters and the lowest sort of race-course toughs; a world in which your six-day-a-week hunting man could quote Xenophon or Horace with the greatest ease, and write a letter to his moneylender in polished Palladian prose; a world in which the most dutiful son thought nothing of 'post-obiting' his well-loved father – in other words, raising a loan on his head at a rate of interest which depended on the lender's opinion of the father's soundness in wind and limb.

Even 'our hero', as Francis Raby is described by his admiring biographer, attempted to enter into a transaction of this kind; and was offered very unfavourable terms because 'Your father, sir, is, I understand, a very regular liver, entering but little into dissipations of the town . . . I think, Mr Raby, he'll hold for a long tug.' Nothing came of the business; and Raby was luckier than Mr Newland, who was so unwise as to call out publicly in the ring at Newmarket: 'What odds will anyone bet me that I don't win the Derby in four years after my old aunt dies?' His aunt got to hear of it, and he lost a hundred thousand pounds, which went to hospitals and Sunday schools. 'It is a good lesson,' we are gravely told, 'to young gentlemen who attempt to post-obit their relations.'

Nimrod, naturally enough, was passionately interested in other people's money, because he had such a job to pay his own bills; and on almost every page of *The Life of a Sportsman* we find evidence of his interest in the cost of living in so far as it affected his microcosmos of lords, lordlings and squires. We learn, for example, that champagne cost sixteen shillings a bottle and claret twelve; that young men at Oxford needed an allowance of at least six hundred a year; that a pair of leaders for a four-in-hand cost four hundred guineas and a pair of wheelers three hundred – so that you drove down to Ascot in your coach behind seven hundred and fifty pounds' worth of horseflesh; and that if the horses you fancied happened to be dappled greys, which were very much in fashion, it cost you a hundred a year in *soap* to keep them clean. A good hunter, fit to go with the Pytchley or the Quorn, set you back about five hundred pounds at Tattersalls; you needed eight of them, and if you rode hard enough you killed two or three each season.

It is easy to understand that a man could be almost pitied for possessing such a 'comparatively limited' income as ten thousand a year!

But the social historian will find in these pages other things to interest him than these illuminating sidelights on Meltonian finance. He will find contemporary sketches of Eton and Christchurch, Bibury Races, with the Prince of Wales (later George IV) running his own horse there, a full-length portrait of the famous Mr Meynell of the Quorn and a dozen other Masters of Foxhounds, a picture of a parliamentary election, and a whole gallery of huntsmen, coachmen, and queer sporting characters drawn from the life – including, incidentally, that remarkable person Captain Barclay who for a wager walked a thousand miles in a thousand hours over Newmarket race-course. Best of all, perhaps, is Nimrod's account of 'The Road' at a time when Mr MacAdam's invention was beginning to revolutionize travel (the London to Edinburgh mail-coach did the journey in sixty-two hours instead of the previous eighty-two). The improvement in the surface doubtless made travel more comfortable for ordinary folks, but it by no means reduced the danger to the young Meltonians who were determined to let slip no opportunity of breaking their necks: they blessed the names of Telford and MacAdam and drove faster still. One cannot but sympathize with the anonymous old gentleman of whom Nimrod remarks *en passant* that he promised to pay for champagne, both on the course at Ascot and at dinner, for the four days of the meeting, on condition that he was not upset either in going or returning.

The truth of the matter is, of course, that the harum-scarum young toffs who bowled along the roads in 1800 without much regard for their own necks or anybody else's were a manifestation of much the same sort of exuberance as the greasy youths in sports cars who terrorized the quiet lanes twenty years ago. In both cases there was a kind of aristocracy of speed. The crack of a whip, the rattle of hoofs, an oath or two, the smell of saddle soap and sweaty horses; or the yowl of an open exhaust, a screech of tyres, and a whiff of Castrol R; and the proletarian wayfarer jumped for his life into the hedge. *Plus ça change.* But in one respect at least the Meltonians had better airs and graces. These hard-drinking, hard-riding, hard-driving, insensitive young devils (it is not without significance that they spoke of their horses as 'cattle') were capable of a wit and polish in their discourse which would have left their modern counterparts utterly tongue-tied. The Greek and Latin which had been beaten into them at Eton, Harrow, Winchester and Westminster did not quite desert them in the hunting-field. Peter

Beckford, of whom it was said that 'he would bag a fox in Greek, find a horse in Latin, inspect his stables in Italian, and direct the economy of his kennels in excellent French' had set the classical fashion; and that curious poet William Somervile, who composed blank verse about hound-management in the seventeen forties and of whom Dr Johnson remarked tolerantly that he wrote quite well for a gentleman, filled his pages with mythological allusions even when he was describing the duties of a whipper-in. It is a fact that John Mytton, half-crazed with delirium tremens and half-dead from the burns which he inflicted on himself when he set his nightshirt afire to cure a hiccough, frequently quoted with pedantic correctness from Horace, Sophocles and the New Testament in Greek. Likewise, 'our hero', Francis Raby, although he often played truant from his lessons to go ferreting or badger-baiting, is liable to quote a dozen 'good authors', including Homer and Shakespeare, whenever he writes to his friends to tell them about a hunting-run. This, surely, is one of the most enchanting contradictions of Nimrod's time. I suppose the Meltonians in their heyday were the toughest collection of young daredevils, with the exception perhaps of the Parachute Regiment, which has ever come together in England; and yet as they galloped hell-for-leather over the wide grassfields and the awful black fences of Leicestershire they sometimes made excellent Latin puns! One Mr Horn, for example, who jumped a tall bullfinch and nearly fell into a sawpit on the other side of it, was asked by a companion who galloped beside him. 'Why did not you look before you leapt?' A wag answered for him in the words of Horace – '*Nemo mortalium omnibus horis sawpit*'.

That swift pun, made not at the dinner-table over the port but in the middle of a fast and furious foxhunt, is the sort of thing which leavens and lightens the rather port-winey atmosphere of the period which Nimrod describes for us. I like it as much in its different way, as the Pytchley huntsman's comment when he jumped clean over a parson floundering in a deep brook: 'His reverence swims like a cork; but never mind him; this is only Friday, and he won't be wanted till Sunday.'

They were polished and tough, cruel and elegant, brave as lions and thoughtless as butterflies, these foxhunting gentry with their spindly legs and their queer, peaky faces peering out between the absurd high collars up to their ears. Nimrod describes them faithfully because he loved them and was blind to their faults. Even 'our hero', who was meant to represent the flower and perfection of the English sportsman, appears to us very far from a paragon in these pages. I therefore refrain from recommending the book to political prigs and puritans, who will make themselves very unhappy deploring the waste, the wantonness and the extravagance of a world which is now as dead as the dodo, and who will be unable to enjoy a single racy paragraph without asking sternly where the ten thousand a year came from. But to all who believe in cakes and ale, and who can taste ginger hot i' the mouth still, I prescribe *The Life of a Sportsman* on the simple grounds that it is good fun. By all means look fair and square at Nimrod's fantastical little world, and see it against its sombre backcloth of the Enclosures and the dark satanic mills. Remember Cobbett's half-starved labourers, the girls working in the turnip-fields 'as pale as ashes and as ragged as colts'. Don't forget the cruelty – of breaking a badger's teeth, for example, and then setting the young hounds on him to give them practice for tearing up a fox. Take all these things into account, but do not let them blind you altogether to the wit, the grace, the fun, and the wild crazy courage which lights these pages now and then. The Meltonians had a million faults, among which you may or may not include their absolute monomania for breaking their necks. They were as wanton as weeds, ungoverned wild weeds strangely blossoming in the ordered fields of our history. They were selfish, drunken, socially useless if you like; but when they were asked how in God's name they managed to get across those huge breakneck ox-fences they answered gaily, 'We send our hearts over first and then follow them in the best way we can.' And I, for one, can forgive them everything for that.

Introduction to The Life of a Sportsman

My grandfather was an able surgeon, who nevertheless functioned as what we nowadays call a G.P. in the small town of Moreton-in-Marsh, in the Cotswolds. He was mad on foxhunting, which is why he preferred a country practice with its modest rewards to the life of a prosperous surgeon in London. He kept a diary, of which I have only the last volume – January 1904 up to the 16th May. *A lovely day but felt very bad . . . went for a drive in the afternoon.* He died that evening.

The entries are mostly very terse and factual, but it is a fascinating document all the same. When my grandfather went his round, he either drove in a dog-cart or rode his mare. (Did he carry his instruments in the usual black bag or did he fit up some sort of Surgeon's Saddlebag, I wonder?) He kept a large-scale map in his surgery in which he pinned little flags with the time of day written on them, e.g. 'noon', 'early afternoon', '4.30 p.m.'. These indicated where he might be found at those hours. If Lady Redesdale had a pain in her tummy she sent her groom galloping to the doctor's house at Moreton, where he consulted the map, then galloped off to intercept the doctor at, let's say, Bourton-on-the-Hill.

Three days a week, in winter, you'd have had a job to catch him. He hunted with the North Cotswold, the Heythrop and the Warwickshire. On these days he drew in his diary a formalized, cocky looking, prick-eared fox bearing the letters 'N.C.', 'H' or 'W' upon its brush. I imagine the Cotswold squires went pretty hard in the nineteen hundreds; there seems to have been an awful lot of what the sporting writers called 'grief' –

'*Nice gallop to Bourton Woods, fairly raced there . . . Col. Savage met with bad accident, fractured pelvis? took him to Lord Gainsborough's . . . Dicky Samuda broke his collar-bone . . .* '

'*Met at Wolford Wood . . . a nice fine day, plenty of galloping . . . Lord Willoughby in terrible temper . . . Mr R^d Arkell met with nasty accident (concussion) . . .* '

The then Lord Willoughby de Broke was the Master of the Warwickshire. He was famous for his temper, and it must have been specially frightful on that occasion for my grandfather to record it in his diary.

The Arkells are still a well-known farming family in the Cotswolds. They seem to have been somewhat accident-prone. I find many references to their broken bones in my grandfather's diary.

It must have been a comfort to have a first-class surgeon handy, when you were going hard over that country of big stone walls.

But now, alas, it was a case of 'Physician, heal thyself'. The brief apprehensive entries creep gradually into the diary, intrusive among the foxhunting notes and the professional memoranda. '*Went to see Nurse at Hospital with typhoid, very bad . . . self poorly*' . . . '*Feeling very seedy . . . Operated on Mrs T. for periosteal abscess . . .*' '*My weight 9st 10*' (a month previously it had been 10st 4). '*Mr Styles came, we talked about Lady Northwick's operation . . . feeling v. sick*' . . . '*Lady N. sent me 2 trout, went to see her, good recovery, self very seedy and depressed.*'

With Zena in 1964 and (*right*) Zena's foal.

Tewkesbury Abbey and (*below*) Church Street; the projecting gable on the left is the John Moore Countryside Museum.

Each day he jotted down his own symptoms; and now and then a tentative diagnosis preceded by ??.

He went to London, to see the specialists who were also his professional friends. One tried a 'Rest Cure' – '*Bed for 1 Week*' which he hated. Another sent him abroad, to the South of France, when the mistral blew and it was 'a real purgatory' which he put up with for a fortnight; then, sick, apprehensive, and *'vilely upset in temper'* like Lord Willoughby de B. he came home to the house and the horses and the countryside he loved. '*Very glad to get there . . . found everything all right . . . and nice!!!*'

Just before the season ended he had one last day on 'Bren' his precious mare. I daresay she wondered at the lightness of him. '*Weight*' he'd noted in his diary '*9st 5*'.

'*A very fine day . . . Hounds ran to Heythrop from Barton Grove, plenty of galloping . . . rode my dear little mare after 2 months absence from saddle . . .*'

That was the last time he put his foot in the stirrup. A few drives in the dogcart on the loveliest of spring days –

'*There's one more May to scant our mortal lot*' wrote Housman when he saw the blossom fading. When the petals blew away that spring it was the last spring blossoming for my grandfather. 'Lovely day' he wrote, again and again, wistfully. Then upon the 16th the mortal lot of May days was all used up and expended, for John Moore, foxhunter and Fellow of the Royal College of Surgeons.

Birmingham Mail, 17 December 1965

Accurate hunting terminology was not a matter which would ever have troubled John, and he would have laughed at me for my purist view that 'pink coat' is quite unacceptable (it was merely an affectation favoured by a few Victorian foxhunters); also 'cubbing' (for 'cub-hunting'), 'whip' (for 'whipper-in') and so on. Such inconsequential pedantry would doubtless appear ridiculous to the majority of readers, and it is only because I AM a purist where hunting phrases are concerned that I venture to criticize mere trivialities in what is otherwise almost incomparable prose.

COUNTRY LIFE

Let Nature be your teacher
WORDSWORTH

In *Midsummer Meadow*, one of the most evocative of his later novels, John has described the haunting loveliness of the Beautiful Place. It was I who so-named it, when we were very young. I suppose that I was about six or seven years old, and to me it was a magical spot of pure delight, particularly in springtime and summer when it was blue with the incomparable blue of a mass of forget-me-nots.

Little more than a decade later I was walking up this same river bank with John, following the Wye Valley Otterhounds, and – Philistine that I was! – quite forgetting those mis-named forget-me-nots and the magic of the Beautiful Place in the exhilaration of the music of hounds as they drove on upstream on the fresh drag of an otter.

Now, with the nostalgia of advancing years, I recall vividly that enchanted and enchanting Beautiful Place in a Gloucestershire stream – 'too pleasant to be looked on, save only on holy days', as good old Izaak Walton wrote, himself a man who loved rivers.

'Of course it's otters,' said Hazel patiently from her green shade, 'but they've got babies.'

'You've seen them?' In all his sixty-six years this glimpse had been denied him.

She slid down the sloping branch and stood at his side.

'Yes. I'll show you. They live in the Beautiful Place.'

'The Beautiful Place?'

'I've always called it that,' she said, and led him through the long dewy grass to a bend, almost a loop, where a semi-circle of willows enclosed a still deep pool, with gravelly shallows above it and a narrow neck of tumbling water at its tail. The doctor, who of course had long ago mapped in his mind every contour and landmark in the microcosmos which was Midsummer Meadow, The Owl Tree, Pigeon Willow, Tadpole Hollow, Ragged Robin Corner and so on, knew this as the Six Willows; but Hazel's childish name served it as well. A bank of water forget-me-not, its saxe-blue softened by the dusk, ran all round the bend, with soldierly yellow irises standing up among it. Later in the year, he knew, there would be dark purple stains of loosestrife, and pink spikes of flowering rush, and a tapestry of rosy willow-herb along the top of the bank. It was certainly the Beautiful Place.

They crouched down together among the meadowsweet, the old man and the young girl, and they waited.

It was so still that they could hear the tiniest minnow breaking the surface. A grasshopper-warbler set up his chirruping far away; a moorhen clucked on the river; upstream some big wings creaked as the swans took off laboriously; moths passed unseen with a flutter that was only just a sound. How much more than that *she* heard the doctor could only guess; she sat beside him tense and eager, lips parted, hardly seeming to breathe.

A small yellowy-green frog came into their ken, plopping noisily. Hazel's hand went out to it as if she would command even the little amphibian to be still. Her fingers enclosed it, and the doctor thought he had never before seen a creature handled so gently; even he, aware as he was that to these tender things we were rough pachyderms, our thumbs nutmeg-graters upon their fearfully-trembling bodies, even he could not pick up a frog so tenderly. Hazel put it down in the grasses beside her, turned to him, and smiled.

And then, suddenly, the otters were in the stream less than ten yards away from them. It was so swift a coming that it was more like a kind of manifestation; neither of the watchers saw whence they came. There were two big ones and three cubs, five streaks of quicksilver. They raced to the tail of the pool, turned on their sides as they went about, and began to play an elaborate game of follow-my-leader up and down the stream.

It was more than a game. It was a mazy dance, a ballet wildly beautiful, performed so swiftly that the doctor's eyes could scarcely follow it. So swift indeed were these streamlined creatures that often they would be splashing at the head of the pool before their tangled wakes had subsided at the tail of it. As the game went on the whole pool became a turbulence of silver; and the otters were black shapes among it, appearing and disappearing here, there and everywhere, now a dark flat head, now a broad flat rudder, now a whaleback arched in readiness for the dive.

In this dance-game there was humour as well as grace. Between the big otters, at any rate, there was a subtle interplay of jest and riposte as if on their otter-level they sparred like Benedick and Beatrice, but without words. It was lovely, mysterious, weird; and yet, thought the doctor, there were scientists who believed that animals in their behaviour were no more than a complex of conditioned reflexes, puppets dancing to nature's tune whenever she elected to pull the strings. A hungry dog salivates; cut out a bit of its brain; show it some food; it still salivates; cut out some more brain; it ceases to salivate; and hey presto, ladies and gentlemen, I have demonstrated to you the precise part of the cortex which operates this particular reflex and if you will keep me adequately supplied with dogs I will guarantee to provide you with a mechanistic explanation of every single aspect of the animal's behaviour . . .

If Pavlov could have watched these otters! thought the doctor.

As suddenly as it had begun, the dance-game ended. It finished with a swirling grand finale, a ring-a-ring-a-roses nosetip-to-tail, fantastic, unearthly; and then the pool went still. The silvery ripples raced themselves to a standstill; the blurry moon and the half-drowned stars took their proper stations again; tree-shadows sharpened. The three cubs, like little dogs, lay on the surface close together; the big otters crawled up the bank, sleek and shining, and for a moment or two paused there. They were not more than twenty feet away; and the doctor heard Hazel catch her breath. He glanced at her, and saw that she was translated, transfixed. An ecstasy of love and wonder possessed her. She was tremulous with love and wonder. '*Sharper do they see, more aware are they . . .*' He took his eyes from the otters for a few seconds – though he had never had wild unhunted otters so close – and watched Hazel instead. She was oblivious of him and of all about her; and he somehow understood that all her senses and perceptions were projected towards the creatures in the pool; she had long ceased to be a watcher of the dance, she had become a participant. She was *being otter*, she was feeling the cool creamy surge on her own skin, the tang of the bursting bubbles, the hardness of water and the softness of air; she was smelling the sweet river-smell, seeing the dark darting underwater shapes and the bright scatter of spray, knowing the frenzy and the fury and the wild delight . . . He understood because he himself before now had so projected himself; he had launched himself into the teeth of a nor'-wester with the wild geese in winter, his spirit storm-tossed as their bodies, he had watched a stoat with a rabbit and had been for a split second both hunter and hunted, had known both the cruel triumph and the pain.

But whereas he had blundered into that other-world of the senses, too coarse for it, too obtuse, sensually a pachyderm, Hazel looked now as if she had taken one clean leap like the otter's dive, into the pool. She was there with them, he was sure; she was with them wholly. There was no magic here but love and sensibility; though, Heaven knew, that was magic enough.

There was a scurry – perhaps he had stirred or Hazel, trembling, had moved the grasses; the otters went, and it was a vanishing, just as their arrival had been like a manifestation. The noises of the night, so long unheard, were back again; a raucous barn-owl, a cockchafer's hum, the frogs' queer mechanical song. The doctor, easing himself up, was sharply aware of reality in the shape of a pain across his loins: his old lumbago. Hazel brushed the dew off her skirt vigorously, and by that brisk action became an ordinary girl again. Neither spoke; but they looked at each other and smiled.

Midsummer Meadow

An aviator himself during the War, when he was a pilot in the Fleet Air Arm, John identified himself with the sea-birds and their remarkable powers of flight which can never be equalled by the invention of mere man. And this interest in 'The Way of a Bird in the Air' remained with him after the War was over and he had the opportunity to ponder such matters, and (as always with him) marvel at the wonderful works of nature.

And now, some grey day in November, the great winds begin to blow that bring down from the north what my old Colonel used to call the 'foreign duck', as opposed to the locally-bred ones: the little teal with their shrill short whistle, the widgeon crying like lost souls, the odds-and-sods as he described them, chance wayfarers, golden-eye, shelduck, shovellers, rare pintails, goosander, merganser, smew. The Colonel shot them all impartially, as he would have shot a mermaid or brought down a witch off her broomstick, and he ate them all whether they were accounted edible or not; he held that if a thing was a duck you could eat it, and somehow he masticated the merganser which unwisely flew over his head at dusk (looking a bit like a ragged old witch) as he waited by the river for the first of the white-fronted geese riding upon a storm of early October.

These storms of the late autumn sometimes bring us odds-and-sods which not even the Colonel could have eaten: for the currents of the air have their flotsam and jetsam as the sea's do, and the Colonel, who attracted rare birds to himself as to a magnet, once picked up a dead bittern in his fields and a few days later a moribund little auk. Although he knew the name and the habits of every bird that bred in our district, he could never be bothered to look up in the books, if he had any, these strangers, foreigners as he called them rather on the principle that niggers begin at Calais. So the bittern, to him, was 'a sort of outlandish heron' and the little auk was 'a kind of perishing sea-parrot, if you ask me'. They were duly displayed in the Swan, the bittern dead and the little auk nearly so, for the Colonel had been trying unsuccessfully to feed it on bread and milk. On another occasion he came hobbling into the bar with a sack over his shoulder. It contained a live gannet which he had found sitting exhausted beside the brook which ran through his meadows. It was covered with blood, not its own but the Colonel's, for its sharp beak had drilled a neat hole in his forearm through his coat. Having demonstrated it to his cronies he bore it to the police-station, as if he were giving it in charge for assault and battery, and the next day the Inspector took it by car, in a sack, to the nearest Zoo, where it died.

This was to be expected; for the gannets and other sea-birds which are overtaken and blown inland by untimely storms have generally run out of fuel and it is very difficult to persuade them to eat and so restore the supply. Not long ago a whole migration of Leech's Petrels was swept out of its course, and scores of the birds, dead or dying, were picked up in the West Midlands. Three fell in our village and were cossetted by schoolboys, but there was really no hope of saving them. Stray gannets reach us almost every autumn and these are generally reported as 'an albatross' or 'a cross between a wild goose and a swan'. Last year we had two, which the village schoolmaster tried hard to revive with fish. He even sent his boys down to the river to catch dace and bleak for them; he sacrificed the goldfish which somebody had won at the October Fair; he sent to the fishmonger at Elmbury for pounds of herrings. But it was no good. Each of the gannets weighed 4½ lbs., which James Fisher tells me is the critical weight for exhausted gannets: if they are as light as that they are almost sure to die. Number One did so immediately, putting its head between its wings, burying its long slate-coloured beak in its soft feathers, and expiring with dignity and deliberation. Number Two ate a few herrings but was very choosy and always refused any that had been kept from the night before. It stayed alive for three days, then ate one goldfish, vomited, stood on tiptoe and spread its great wings to their full six feet, became for a moment as a bird of heraldry, and thus theatrically took its leave of the world.

It strikes me as strange that these powerful birds are so often blown out of their courses: for they are better aeronauts, I should think, than the buzzard or the kite or the great golden eagle itself. When they plunge, falling plummet-wise for two or three hundred feet upon a shoal of fish, they go at least as fast as a stooping peregrine; the splash as they enter the water is like the impact of a little bomb. Their nearest breeding-place to Gloucestershire is on Grassholm, off the coast of Wales; but the gannets which accidentally visit us are unlikely to have come from there, and have probably lost their way while on southern migration from Scotland. Oddly enough they do not always arrive in stormy weather. One was picked up dead in our village during a period of autumnal calm. Unlike the others, it was plump and in the pink of condition; it had broken its neck. Surely a migrating gannet would fly too high to collide with power-cables or telegraph-wires; so perhaps it was hit by the wing of an aeroplane, possibly one of those jets which howl through our skies like wild witches in a sabbath nightmare.

I wish I knew more about sea-birds. We inlanders rarely get a chance to observe them, and the one glorious opportunity I had – when I was at sea during the war – was largely wasted owing to the tiresome whims of my Lords of the Admiralty, who always ordered my ship somewhere else just as I was settling down happily to study fulmars, gannets or puffins. Gulls, of course, were always with us, even during an action they would cry their pitiful lament about the ship: flying close alongside they would turn towards us their bright-eyed, hard-bitten faces, the faces of seafarers all the world over. The petrels too, Mother Carey's chickens, used to follow us far out into the Atlantic, when we were looking for submarines; Mother Carey, by the way, is supposed to be a corruption of *Mater cara*, and indeed the French call these far-flying chickens *Oiseaux de Notre Dame*.

What voyagers, what globe-trotters the sea-birds are, some of which breed in one hemisphere and spend the next six months in the other! I have flow from a carrier in mid-Atlantic, ranging a hundred miles or so about her, and have returned to her with the aid of a gyro-compass, a homing beacon, radar, an observer's skilful plotting, and now and then a bit of sheer luck. But one day, when my ship was 2000 miles from the nearest land, a small bird called a phalarope, not much bigger than an English thrush, plonked down on our flight-deck, remained with us for an hour or two, and then took off in the direction of Greenland. On another occasion I saw a whole flock of these small greyish birds riding on the huge Atlantic rollers, and greatly I envied them, for I was nearly out of fuel, like those exhausted gannets, and my Swordfish would not have floated if I had come down in the sea.

Sometimes when I was flying in formation (which I hated and never found easy) I used to envy the knots. These gregarious waders fly in flocks five or ten thousand strong, and the flocks weave themselves into strange serpentine patterns in the sky. The birds are packed densely, wingtip to wingtip, yet when one turns all turn. There are no collisions, there is no confusion, and in a split second the whole immense cohort has changed direction, often simultaneously in both the vertical and horizontal planes. If the sun happens to be shining you see the light-pattern alter on their wings and as they turn the whole flock blinks a semaphore-flash of white. How do they manage, so many of them, to turn so quickly? By sharper eyesight, I suppose, and swifter-acting reflexes, than we earthbound ones can even imagine.

The way of a bird in the air, which was one of the things too wonderful for the author of the Book of Proverbs, is likewise too wonderful for me. I shall never understand how the Pacific golden plover navigates itself across 2000 miles of ocean without a single landmark on its route; how the greater shearwater after a trip round the Atlantic by way of Greenland, Iceland and Cape Verde finds its way back to the tiny island of Tristan da Cunha where it breeds. But if an amateur naturalist may make a guess, mine would be that most birds fly by sight and topographical memory; not by instinct or sixth sense. They may *inherit* memories of temperatures and prevailing winds, which would be a kind of instinct. But fog and low cloud always beats them, as it beat airmen before radar was invented. So I think they navigate by visual means – even across the wastes of the ocean. After all, what to me may seem an illimitable forest of undistinguishable trees is to a jungle tracker as full of landmarks as a familiar street. The Western Desert (which Sir Winston Churchill is said to have described as 'acres and acres of arid austerity – how Stafford would have loved it!') is to the Arab's eye criss-crossed with well-marked tracks and divided into clearly-defined areas by the wave-patterns of wind-blown sands. And I flew so much over the sea during the war that I am sympathetic with the theory so well summarised by Mr W. R. Phillipson in his *Birds of a Valley*: 'It is possible that to oceanic birds the sea is no more featureless than a landscape is to us. A bird which lives continuously on the sea may well be sensitive to changes in its salinity or warmth, and look upon its currents as we do upon rivers, and may even distinguish the plants and animals of its surface layers, as we do between a forest and a desert.'

If you have yourself been an aviator, you can get a special interest out of watching birds; you understand some of the complicated problems involved in being airborne which they are conditioned to deal with in the course of their day-to-day affairs. Standing by the river the other evening, waiting for the wild duck, I watched four swans take off on their short evening flight to the pool three miles away where they spend the night. They are clumsy birds, almost as clumsy as those old Walrus aircraft which I flew in the Fleet Air Arm, and are obviously underpowered in relation to their weight. They need a long run for their take-off, and preferably a stiff breeze. They retract their undercarriages as soon as they are airborne, big webbed feet are tucked into the fuselage-feathers, and of course when they are landing they lower their undercarriages and apply the air-brakes in their wings. This quickly slows the steep glide, and they finally touch down with the nose held high, as we used to land our aeroplanes on the carrier.

All birds, of course, land and take off into wind, or at least they should do: but young rooks, doing their early solos, sometimes make the same mistakes which inexperienced pilots make and land cross-wind, or hold off too high, stall, and crash. The crash doesn't hurt them much, but it is a blow I think to their self-esteem. They waddle away rather quickly and with an air of pretending that nothing went wrong.

But no birds remain Prunes for long. Very soon they are complete masters of their element, experts in the particular kind of flying for which their build and streamlining best fits them: the humming-bird is a hoverplane, the peregrine and the gannet are dive-bombers, the teal is as manoeuvrable as a single-seater fighter at high speed.

Some birds are aerobatic, notably jackdaws, which seem to perform complicated manoeuvres simply for fun – as indeed tumbler pigeons do, and peewits during their evening flight just before dusk. As far as I can see the peewits go in for half-rolls, one to the right, one to the left, executed in rapid succession. The tumbler pigeons put themselves into a kind of spin. But the jackdaws, especially when they are teasing some other bird such as a buzzard, perform correct flick-rolls, stall turns (just in front of the buzzard's beak) and even rolls off the top of a loop. I have never yet seen a bird do a complete loop and suppose it to be impossible; if so this is one up to me. I once for a bet drank a whole pint of beer without spilling more than a few drops of it, holding the tankard in one hand and the joystick in the other, while I pulled an old Moth over in a very tight loop. Let me add that there is no special skill in this; it is something to do with centripetal force; and any pilot can do it if he is prepared to put up with the subsequent attack of hiccups.

I suppose the most exciting thing, for any airman who watches birds, is the spectacle of a falcon tearing down upon its prey; for here is the fighter-pilot in action, and he obeys exactly the same rules that war taught us – seize the advantage of height, get above your foe, dive to the attack, approach from behind. But even the falcons make mistakes sometimes. I once saw a hen peregrine stoop at a low-flying flock of duck which were crossing a lake not ten feet above the water. The peregrine came down 'like a bat out of hell', as we should have said in the war, struck one of the duck and tore some feathers out of it, but badly misjudged her height above the water, which is easy to do in a dead calm because an airman flying over water can only guess his height in relation to ripples or waves. So the peregrine pulled out of her dive much too late and slapped her breast against the water as she did so with a sound like a sharp crack; it must have hurt her badly, for she staggered and nearly stalled as she began to climb away. The moment before she hit the water I felt myself, for a second, to *be* a falcon; I could imagine the huge effort to pull out of the dive, the strong tug of gravity, the strain on the wings and spread-eagled tail, the blackout or grey-out which she must suffer as what pilots call 'g' began to affect her and the blood drained away from the brain. It may have been the effect of that 'g' which caused her to stagger as she rose from the water; but she quickly recovered, and soon her wonderful wings had carried her high into the sky again.

I can understand the fascination of falconry, because of the opportunity it provides to watch a hawk hunting at pretty close quarters, but I never want to possess, least of all to tame, one of these wild and lovely and savage birds. To tame such a feral thing must in any case involve exquisite cruelty; but these torments were devised at a time when bear-baiting was regarded as light entertainment and to witness the hanging, drawing and quartering of a criminal was the equivalent of going up for the Cup-Final; so nobody was likely to worry about the miseries inflicted upon a hawk. In any case falconry was an important industry. A good hawk was a valuable commodity; a great lord's falconer was a senior member of his household staff. The quaint terms used in connexion with the sport were familiar to everybody and indeed had become common usage, as we quickly learn when we listen to almost any play by Shakespeare. How beautifully he used these terms! For instance, when Othello says of Desdemona:

> *If I do prove her haggard,*
> *Though that her jesses were my dear heart-strings,*
> *I'd whistle her off, and let her down the wind*
> *To prey at fortune.*

or when Juliet from her balcony cries out to the dark garden where Romeo lurks hidden from her:

> *O for a falc'ner's voice*
> *To lure this tassel-gentle back again!*

But if I possessed a hawk, I know that before long I should 'whistle her off and let her down the wind' – what a heart-lifting phrase! – for I could never bring myself to confine one. I did, as a matter of fact, for a few days keep a sparrow-hawk. It had been injured, possibly by a keeper's shot, and it couldn't fly; I thought its wing might mend if I looked after it. But it perched implacable in its improvised cage, refusing all food, and regarding me with bleak hatred out of the most beautiful eyes in all nature. Then it drooped; and with horror, all one day, while I tried to tempt it with morsels, I saw the beauty of those eyes fading, they became lack-lustrous, a film crept over them, and my only tassel-gentle – but far from gentle, tameless to the end – made a brief flutter to the corner of the cage, flopped down, and died there. I know I couldn't have done anything to save her; she would perhaps have died sooner in the wild. But I was uncomfortably aware that she died hating the cage and hating me. I never want to see a sick hawk again; nor a healthy one save when it has the freedom of the whole wide sky, when its lovely wings like oar-blades cleave the air, bearing it so swiftly down the wind to prey at fortune.

Down the wind, some night in the neighbourhood of Hallowe'en, come the wild geese which the Colonel loved, the first small V-shaped gaggles on their way to the feeding-grounds called the Dumbles, where Peter Scott has established the Severn Wildfowl Trust as their sanctuary. They are mostly white-fronts, with a few greylags, and generally they pass high overhead and offer few chances to the gunners who go out at dusk or dawn in the marshes and meadows by the river. The Colonel used to wait for them with Sweep at his side, and even in his later days, when he became too deaf to hear the clamour in the sky, he still went goose-shooting and used Sweep as his spotter, for the Labrador had ears keen enough for two. The Colonel would simply watch the dog; and only when Sweep cocked his head and looked up into the sky would he raise his own grizzled head and turn his eyes in the direction in which Sweep's long muzzle was pointing. Then perhaps he would catch a glimpse of the gaggle going over; and if they were in range a glimpse was all he needed, for he was the best shot I have ever known. This curious partnership of dog and man once resulted in a bag of three white-fronts, fetched down out of a stormy night-sky when scuds of black cloud were blowing across the moon.

But most of us do not get a sight of this vanguard of the big goose-flocks which will come later; they are a sound in the sky, only a far faint chatter which grows louder, louder, until it becomes a kind of yelping, as if there were ghostly hounds up there in the wind. A moment later it is gone; but although the yelping is so brief, a matter of seconds only, it is surprising how many people hear it, how many men come into the pub that night with their coat-collars turned up and a boding of winter about them, saying: 'The geese be going over . . . Maybe we'll get some snow . . .'

Come Rain, Come Shine

The oasis was unoccupied, and Ralph prepared to bivouac for the night. He was posting sentries when Sergeant Graves, looking up sharply into the sky, caught his arm with a whispered intense 'Hark, sir!'

Ralph stood frozen-still, listening. Then he heard: 'Honk, honk, honk . . .' A skein of wild geese was passing overhead towards the riverine marshes, and their cries came out of the dark heavens like the voices of ghosts, invisible flying things.

Ralph remembered the geese that came up the Wye at home in winter-time; long ribbons of them, in rough weather, stretching from horizon to horizon, passing between cold moon and frozen earth with the eerie cries of disembodied spirits; and suddenly a remark of Sergeant Graves's startled him by the quaintness of the idea.

'There's England flying overhead,' said the sergeant.

Dixon's Cubs

I think a countryman can best be defined as a person for whom at least one sheet of the largest-scale ordnance map has a special and personal meaning; for whom those arbitrary symbols represent something real and vivid, so that he can say, Here is the under-keeper's cottage in the clearing, here the little weir where the cannibal trout lies, here the village shop at which boys buy catapult-elastic and toffee-apples, here the upland where the pasque-flowers and the fly-orchids grow, here the hedgerow where there was a red-backed shrike's larder last summer . . . These things, trifles in themselves, make up the Countryman's England; which is something indefinable and impossible to analyse, being not one thing but a mixture of many. It is woods, fields, hills, rivers; it is foxes, fish, pheasants, hares; it is sunshine, rain, frosts, great winds, autumn mists, April and June and December; it is dogrose, meadowsweet, comfrey, coltsfoot, the smell of new-mown hay, poppies in corn; it is horses, rods, guns, spaniels; it is cricket-matches, birds'-nesting, duck-flighting, talk in the pubs at evening, village halls, lovers in a lane; it is ploughs, steaming cattle in a market, hedge-laying, sheep silver-wet after a storm; it is all these things and many more. But it has nothing whatever to do with flags, patriotism, the red-white-and-blue, politics, out-posts of Empire, and Britannia ruling the waves.

A fragment, then, of the six-inch ordnance map, a sheet picked at random from Devon or Dorset, Sussex or Shropshire, will stand as well as anything else for this secret and indescribable thing, compounded so variously of fishing-rods and mowing grass, cricket-bats and ploughs, bread-and-cheese and ragged robin, which we call the Countryman's England. Only the countryman, who possesses (though he may be merely the tenant of the meanest cottage) a 'place' which he may call his own, – only he, I think, can know a little bit of England so intimately that a sheet or a half-sheet of the large-scale map becomes, as it were, the record of his work and play, his walks, his rides, his sport, his trivial adventures, in fact his life. And if by chance he has to leave his 'place', the little bit of country which he has made his own, if he goes to live in a town or travels abroad, the map will always keep its special meaning for him and he will never forget it. At Ceuta in Spanish Morocco I met such a man. He was second-mate on a dirty old collier, and he came from Devon, where his father was tenant of a farm. The chief decoration of his cabin was a plan of his farm, torn out of an auctioneer's particulars of sale, which he had pinned to the wall between a picture of a voluptuous young woman, cut out of *La Vie Parisienne*, and a faded photograph of his father on a fat pony. He had written on the plan the names of all the fields; but I think he need not have done so, for he would never forget them. He loved to stand in front of the map and point out with his finger the scenes of remembered happenings. 'You see that little twisting footpath running down through the wood called Foxwood – well, it's Foxwood on the plan, but the real name is Folkswood, fairies, I suppose, – anyhow, that's the path where we used to go courting. A white owl used to sit on a gatepost there, and sometimes he'd scare the wenches when he flapped past them like a ghost. And the bats used to squeal and squeak in the air on hot evenings. That bank on the left is full of rabbit-burys and primroses. Down at the bottom of the lane a queer old gypsy-fellow used to live in a sort of tumbledown caravan . . .'

And so on. It became a bit boring after a time, if one didn't know the places he was talking about. All his fellow-officers on the ship had grown heartily sick of it, and it was a friendly joke on board that when Tom Spry started talking about his father's farm it was time to say you'd got to go up on the bridge. I was a passenger, so I had no valid excuses; and I had to put up with it, in rough weather, all the way to Alicante. He'd go on for hours about the fine crops his father grew, in this field or that one, or the places where he'd found young cuckoos in small birds' nests, while I stood politely beside the map and tried to keep my feet while the floor heaved up and down. I became very tired of that Devon coombe, and the covert called Foxwood; but all the same, it's pleasant to think of that stained and crumpled yet terribly precious map going about the world with Tom Spry, keeping the memories vivid in his mind. I hope he goes back there when he retires from the sea, and finds everything the same as it used to be, the primroses and the rabbit-holes and the white owl still on his gatepost.

This book is like the second-mate's babbling; and I can only hope that the reader, who is sitting in a comfortable armchair and not standing, as I was, with a queasy stomach on a cake-walking deck, will not grow bored with the trivial chronicle of little things which make my map mean much more to me than any other map. These little things, pulled haphazard out of memory like prizes out of a lucky dip, are unimportant in themselves but they make a sort of pattern nevertheless, and the pattern, when you can see it, is England: not the England of the Jingoes and the flag-waggers, but something much more complex, much more secret, and much more precious to Englishmen.

The Countryman's England

THE TOP OF THE HILL

We'll begin at the top of Brensham Hill, because from there you will get a good idea of the kind of country in which our village is set. This is the land which has made and moulded us. Look north, south, east and west, and you shall see as it were the four corner-stones of our character: the ancient foundations of our way of thinking and living, our wisdom, folly, manners, customs, humours, what you will.

Look north, then, where the Avon snakes down from Stratford through the Evesham vale. With the aid of glasses on a very clear day you can just make out the red-brick ordinary-looking small town which people in Patagonia and Pekin have heard of, though perhaps they couldn't name anywhere else in England save London. Shakespeare seems very close when you walk on Brensham Hill. He had friends in this neighbourhood, but a day's good tramp from his home, and just across the river lived one who witnessed his will. You will find yourself wondering, when you see a very old tree, whether he sat in the shade of it; or when you come to a pub, whether he drank there. Now and then on some old labourer's lips a country word or a turn of phrase brings him closer still. For example, we have a word which schoolboys use for the crackly dry stems of the hemlock and the hedge-parsley: 'kecksies', a local word which is heard, I think, nowhere else in England; but Shakespeare puts it into the mouth of the Duke of Burgundy in *Henry the Fifth*:

> *Nothing teems*
> *But hateful docks, rough thistles,* kecksies, *burs . . .*

So, you see, he spoke our speech and thought our thoughts. These our woods and fields, our lanes and rivers, served him as a backcloth for Arden or Athens, Burgundy or Illyria.

Look south, downstream, to the old town of Elmbury standing at the junction of Avon and Severn. Just below the junction is the battlefield called the Bloody Meadow in which the Red Rose went down and the White Rose triumphed on a May day in 1471. By chance a deep-red flower called Cranesbill grows profusely in this meadow; at times it almost covers it; and if you look through strong glasses from the top of Brensham Hill at this patch of English earth on a summer day you will see the dreadful stain upon it, you will see it drenched in Lancastrian blood. After the battle the routed army streamed into Elmbury Abbey for sanctuary, and the young Prince Edward who fell that day is buried there. With him lie the great lords who helped to shape the fortunes of England for three centuries, the makers and unmakers of Kings whose mighty names thunder through the chronicles of Hall and Stow and Holinshed: the Despencers and the De Clares and the Warwicks and the Beauchamps, and the false, fleeting, perjur'd Clarence who met his inglorious end in a butt of Malmsey wine. These old stones and bones give us, I think, a sense of the past: not a knowledge of history (for there are few men in Brensham who could tell you the date of Elmbury's battle nor which side won it) but an acceptance of history, which is much the same thing as a sense of proportion. It accounts, perhaps, for our attitude to the Brensham Bomb and to a couple of wars in a lifetime; but it is not a conscious attitude, it is simply of piece of our background with which we have grown so familiar that we forget it is there, – just as when we go to church at Elmbury we forget the Lords of Old Time who lie all round us and keep us silent company.

And now look east to the strong Cotswolds where rugged shepherds have watched their flocks since 1350. The winds blow cold there, and at night the stars in their courses wheel slowly across an immense sky. The men from being much alone grow taciturn, and their long stride takes a queer rhythm from the slopes of the whaleback hills. Brensham, seven hundred feet high, is itself an outlier of the Cotswolds; so thence, perhaps comes our hillmen's lope, and thence the trick of being silent when we have nothing to say.

Lastly, look west to the Malverns and beyond them to the mountains of Wales. It's not very far across the Severn and the Wye to the dark shut-in valleys and the cold slate villages and the savage Fforest Fawr; it's certainly not too far for a man to go courting if he has a mind to – so if an anthropologist came to Brensham and started to measure our heads he'd discover a fine puzzling mixture of long ones and short ones and betwixts and betweens. And he'd find if he could look inside the heads a compound and amalgamation of Welsh wildness and English sedateness, Border magic and Cotswold common sense. For though we live in a fat and fruitful vale, yet we have a sense of looking out on to the wide waste lands and the mysterious mountains. That's where our occasional turbulence comes from, and the fancy that tried to pen the cuckoo, and our love of singing.

The Blue Field

As children we were fortunate in being given, as birthday or Christmas presents from our parents or the multitudinous aunts which blessed – and sometimes plagued – our childhood, books on animals and Natural History, and these must have influenced us more than a little. In particular I can remember *Eyes and No Eyes*, which John mentions on several occasions in his writings. I can see it now; a smallish, thick green-covered volume; but what I recall most clearly is the title. I think that possibly this book, together with *John's Flowers of the Field*, did more than all the rest to educate that naturally perceptive eye, which is exemplified in such passages as this . . .

The leaves fall, each sort in a different fashion, according to their kind. Birch throws them down in golden handfuls like the sovereigns of Victorian days prodigally cast by some reformed Scrooge. The elm, being so tall and giving its topsails to the strongest winds, streams out on gusty days a comet's tail of little leaves blown far and wide. The beech-leaves are brown already when they fall, and crisp, so that they drop upon the woodland floor with a faint harsh sound; they are reluctant to settle into earth's bosom and stay wakeful, stirring at the least breeze, agitated into dervish-dances like those dust-devils of the African sand.

The oak-leaves cling late, and are ripped off by the north-wester which brings the first snow. The ash-leaves spin down like miniature propellers whirling. The poplars spin too, but with a quicker rotation. The chestnut leaves float. On a still day, in a still churchyard, you can count the seconds as they fall; they are surely the 'falling leaves' which the early fliers imitated when they tried their first daring aerobatics, for they rock with a hammock's motion during their journey to the earth, a quick plunge, a slower ascent, a stall, a spin, a plunge, an ascent, until at last with quite an audible plop they fall on to the wet pavement where they lie so deep that they are over the tops of your shoes as you scuffle through them. So the man who looks after the churchyard must sweep them away, or the rain will turn them to mush, and the old folk next Sunday will grumble and wish for the goloshes which were fashionable in their youth, and the young ones will find a peculiar delight in sliding among them, so that they pile up in wet heaps over the tops of their shoes, – 'Come *along*, Tommy, whatever are you doing, you'll catch your death, with your stockings all soaked, sitting through the sermon . . .'

Come Rain, Come Shine

Egbert had made the bird-table, which fitted close against the sitting-room window. It had a pole with a sort of yard-arm arrangement, designed by Ferdo, from which was hung the lump of suet for the tits. Like everything carpentered by Egbert it had been made to last for a hundred years. He had grumbled, of course, all the time he worked on it. He thought it would encourage the spadgers and other pestses. And so it did; but it afforded Ferdo the greatest pleasure as he watched the starlings which played up like low comedians, and the acrobatic tits which he got to know individually and for which he invented names. A regular attendant was Whisky, one of the black-and-white blackbirds whose nestlings, Ferdo thought, had been destroyed by the Teddy-boys. In the coldest weather there had been rarer, more exciting visitors. One day a nuthatch came, but it found nothing to its liking, and after a quick look round it flew away. Two or three times during January a greater spotted woodpecker, splendidly incarnadined, had alighted upon the lump of fat and pecked away at it for twenty minutes or so. It made a happy morning for Ferdo, when the woodpecker came.

Sometimes he would doze in his chair, and the birds coming to the table would seem to fly in and out of his dreams. This morning, after one of these catnaps, he opened his eyes to see a grey squirrel, bold as brass, rippling towards him across the lawn. Another of those little bastards, another of those pests! He still blamed the grey squirrels for usurping the red ones; they didn't belong to Doddington and they had no right there. They were pests of the woodlands, as mice were pests of the Manor. This one now stopped in the middle of the lawn and cautiously looked around. Ferdo leaned forward and quickly pushed open the window. Then he went to the gun-room and fetched his 12-bore. He slipped in a couple of cartridges, sat himself comfortably in his chair, and took aim.

Just as he was about to pull the trigger, however, the squirrel, sitting up on its hind legs, began to clean its whiskers with its paws. This was so endearing an action that Ferdo could not bring himself to shoot. After a minute or two he laid down the gun. The grey squirrel hopped a bit nearer. Now that he could see it better, Ferdo was amused by its pert and intelligent air. It was less than a dozen yards away, and he could have blown it to smithereens, but he decided not to. Perhaps it intended to rob the bird-table. That would be fun – a squirrel on the window-sill! He remembered that somebody had told him grey squirrels could be tempted by chocolate, so he pottered off and found the remains of a box of Suchard which Susan had given him for Christmas, because it was his favourite kind.

When he came back the squirrel was within a few yards of the bird-table; but it caught sight of him and scurried away. It did not go far, however. It stopped at the edge of the lawn. Ferdo broke up one of the pieces of plain chocolate and put some of it on the bird-table, some on the window sill. He settled down to wait; and soon he went to sleep again. Before long he thought he was dreaming, because he saw the grey squirrel sitting on the bird-table. Perhaps it had made some little sound when it landed there, and this was what had woken him up. He sat very still in his chair, and at last the little beast picked up a morsel of chocolate in its front paws, examined it suspiciously, and began to nibble it. When it had finished it moved an inch or two nearer to the window, and took another piece.

Ferdo was delighted by all this. He had never seen a grey squirrel at such close quarters before. It even came close enough to seize one of the pieces of chocolate which he'd laid on the sill; but just then it must have noticed some slight movement on his part, and it jumped back on to the edge of the bird-table. From that point of vantage, sitting up on its hind legs, ready at any moment to flee if need be, it peered into the room. Its whiskers twitched. The lips drawn back in excitement or curiosity showed the little teeth and gave to its expression the semblance of a smile.

You cheeky little upstart, thought Ferdo, ousting your betters, those beautiful bright red squirrels, from my Doddington woods! They've lived here since long before Domesday Book. Nobody in these parts had *heard* of your kind thirty years ago. . . .

Your betters, I said. But who's to decide what's better or worse in your world of squirrels? Maybe the better squirrel is the one who knows best how to survive in the rough tough world as it is today; the one that's got the most enterprise and the most guts!

Good luck to you, little upstart, thought Ferdo, as the squirrel made up its mind to go home and poured itself almost like a snake over the edge of the bird-table. Come back and see me another day! Then Ferdo dozed, and dreamed and half woke, saw the bird-table was deserted, dozed and dreamed again.

The Waters under the Earth

It is very difficult for us to understand the strange affections and affinities which, from time to time, spring up between domestic creatures of different species; and I doubt if the students of animal behaviour have ever produced a satisfactory explanation of them. I said 'domestic creatures' because it is among them that we have the best chance to observe these odd companionships; but I dare say similar affections occur sometimes in the wild. There are so many tales, some of them painfully sentimental, of different kinds of wild animals associating together in what appears to be a sort of 'friendship' that we cannot dismiss them altogether. Among our own domestic beasts, certainly, most extraordinary 'friendships' arise. Race-horses often make friends with some such beast as a sheep, a goat, a dog, or a cat, and become more or less inseparable from their ill-suited crony. These 'friends' naturally have to go racing along with the horse, travelling in the horse-box, sleeping in the stable. If they are not there, the thoroughbred becomes fratchy and difficult, and possibly does not run a good race. I once heard of a horse – a hunter, not a race-horse – whose special friend was a cat. It used to sit in the manger at feeding time, and if the cat was not there, the hunter would pine and refuse to eat its corn.

Zena's stable companion is a domestic fowl called Henny. She would obviously have a different name, or no name at all, if she were not our *only* hen. It is absurd for anybody to keep a single hen, but this is how it came about. Last September, when we moved to our new house, we discovered this bird wandering about the fields; she'd been there, apparently fending for herself, living on weed-seeds, since the departure of the previous owners in July. She was almost as wild as a partridge; but hunger tamed her, and soon we had her coming to the back door for food. She was a bright chestnut pullet, Rhode Island cross, and before long she started laying little brown eggs for our breakfast. We had decided, before we came to the farm, to give up keeping poultry altogether, and to buy our eggs in the village. However, we couldn't bring ourselves to get rid of Henny or to spoil her uniqueness, as it were, by getting some more fowls. She still lived out, half wild, and faithfully laid an egg a day in a calf-manger, until about Christmas, when she went into a moult. The weather got colder and colder; one night there were 28 degrees of frost; and poor Henny lived through it with no more covering for her pink goosepimply body than a Windmill girl might have. She survived; and by virtue of her fortitude became as it were a Sacred Bird. Obviously we couldn't give away, or kill and eat, so heroic a creature; nor could we bring ourselves to buy half a dozen hens to go with her, for such a dilution of our hen population would reduce her status from that of Henny, our one and only Henny, to that of just another of those blasted fowls.

She got back her feathers and shone, smart and fulvous, in the spring sun. She started laying again. And the next thing she did was to go broody.

Although we had determined not to have any more of her kind we felt that after all her sufferings Henny deserved to have the pleasure of bringing up a family. We got hold of a dozen bantam eggs and put them in a nest for her. She sat on them, devotedly, for thirty-two days, after which we began to wonder why there weren't any bantam chicks (and so did she, so thin by now that her breast-bone was as sharp as a boat's keel). We broke the eggs open and found they were addled.

Did ever ill-luck so relentlessly pursue a bird? The next thing that happens in this melancholy drama is that we go off in search of *some* sort – any sort – of new-born chicks which might be acceptable to the bereaved, or rather the unfulfilled, fowl. The only chicks we can get hold of are some week-old ducklings; never mind, half a dozen ducks are just what we want, how nice they'll look swimming on the mill-stream . . . At the dead of night the ducks were introduced to Henny, and in the morning we found her scratching up the ground in search of worms for them, cluck-clucking and fussing over them, and doing all the things which a hen does for the benefit of her own chickens.

Weeks went by. Henny and the fluffy ducklings became a familiar sight on the lawn. A half-grown rat was discovered, dead, beside the fowl-run where they spend the night. A cat showed an interest in the ducklings and was pecked hard on the nose. What a redoubtable Henny! Then the ducks got bigger and braver and ventured on to the little side-stream where it joins our brook. Henny, hating water, nevertheless paddled to keep them company. She looked about as cheerful as a maiden aunt 'amusing the children' at Weston-super-Mare. One day the ducks, greatly daring, actually swam across the main stream and landed on the other side, loudly week-weeking for mother. Henny, unable to swim but enterprising as ever, flapped her wings three times, took off, flew the stream as precariously as Blériot crossing the English Channel, and made a bumpy landing beside her clamorous ducks on the opposite bank. The ducks then decided to swim back again, and Henny did another uncomfortable solo.

At last the ducks following their nature took more or less permanently to the water, causing such a frightful dichotomy to Henny's mind that we thought she would go out of her wits. Desperate it seemed for company, she took up residence in Zena's loose-box; and there she spends most of the day. She pecks up the oats which Zena spills, scratches in the straw among Zena's feet, and is never in danger of being kicked or trampled. While Zena munches hay, Henny perches on the edge of her manger; and when Zena puts her head over the loose-box half-door to look out, Henny flies up and sits there, a few inches away from her nose.

The Year of the Pigeons

It was soon after the dinner-party at the Daglingworths' that Stephen came down for a weekend, and walking in the woods with him Susan had a strange little adventure. She found a ghost orchis.

On this Sunday morning they had decided for some reason to go a different way which took them right out of their usual territory into the only part of Doddington woods where there was a preponderance of beech over oak.

Now the glossy beech leaves tend to be less destructible and to lie about longer than any other leaves; and as Susan walked upon a thick carpet of them in a glade between the beeches where nothing green could grow, her attention was attracted to a humble-bee's loud buzzing. It was right at her feet, and looking down she spotted this bumble and wondered what it was so excited about; because she didn't, at first, see the flower. She bent down, the bumble flew away, and then she noticed the small undistinguished-looking thing, a plant about four inches high that had a straw-coloured stem without any leaves. Instead of leaves it had two or three little brown bracts attached to it; and the sparse flowers which hung down from it were sad, wishy-washy, pale yellow and pale mauve – but unmistakably orchid-like things.

She had never seen anything like it before, so she called Stephen and he looked down and cried: 'Good God, you must be a witch or something.' Then he told her it was a ghost orchis, and one of the rarest flowers in Britain. It had another, duller name: the Spur-lipped Coralroot. Less than a dozen plants had been seen in the last hundred years; and by a most remarkable chance all but one of them had been found by women!

Stephen said it nearly made him believe in magic; and indeed about the plant itself there seemed to be something magical and mysterious, for while its root remained underground for many years, and got its nutriment with the aid of an associated fungus out of the decaying leaves, the *flower* only poked up its head at long, irregular intervals once every five or six years, perhaps. 'A sort of comet of the plant world!' was how Stephen put it. Obviously the odds were millions to one against anybody finding a ghost orchis, because in the first place it was so rare, in the second it hardly ever showed above ground, and in the third its combination of colours – drab brown, pale yellow, faint mauve – served as a very good camouflage, merging into the leaf-carpet out of which it sprung.

'It's like a ghost in its comings and goings,' said Stephen. 'It's like the flood in your cellar, the waters under the earth, popping up unpredictably. But goodness, what luck you had, what sharp eyes you have, to find it!'

He went down on his knees beside the precious drab egregious thing. He said: 'Smell it,' and Susan crouched down beside him: it smelt of vanilla, faintly and unexcitingly to others than humble-bees.

'Think of this,' said Stephen. 'More people have got themselves close to the summit of Everest than have seen a ghost orchis growing. What you've done is rather like discovering an extra Shakespeare first folio among the junk at a furniture sale, when there are only about sixteen first folios in the world!'

The Waters under the Earth

In the tumult of England's crises there have always been men who have babbled of her green fields, and whose small insistent babbling has made itself heard above the shouts of victorious mobs and the marching and countermarching of soldiers in her wars. Theirs has been a sort of whispered chronicle of little things, a tale told in undertones. It began, I think, on that April morning of showers and sunshine when Chaucer's pilgrims set out along the road to Canterbury and the small birds made melody for them. It went on through all the exciting times when Englishmen were sailing their ships to the ends of the earth, when Drake and Frobisher were beating the Spaniard and Sir Walter Ralegh was looking for El Dorado; for even in that age when poets were decorating their verses with dear-bought words from the Indies and the Americas, Michael Drayton sang the little Warwickshire rivers – 'ev'ry pearl-pav'd ford and ev'ry blue-ey'd deep' – and young Gervase Markham, who wrote the stirring tale of Grenville and the *Revenge*, had time to spare also for a book of *Country Contentments*, about English fields and English weather and the trivial, pleasant things men did with horses and hawks and hounds. Shakespeare too, whose great mind ranged about the world and brought back a Cleopatra from Egypt, an Ariel and a Caliban from the Bermoothes – he never forgot the daisies pied and violets blue, nor the primroses that die unmarried in the cold English spring, nor the March winds that set the woods astir.

> *When daffodils begin to peer,*
> *With heigh! the doxy over the dale.*

and though he might lay his scene in Athens or Illyria, in Venice or Navarre, the English woodlands always crept willy-nilly into it, and the humble homely flowers, and the meadows silver with lady's-smock through which the slow Avon ran from Stratford down to Fladbury and Evesham.

And so the quiet chronicle goes on. While England is at Civil War there is the gentle voice of Izaak Walton, supremely unconcerned, telling of dace and dairymaids; and Richard Franck, trooping with Cromwell, forgets psalm-singing for a while and catches salmon. And Robert Herrick, in the twilight that contains an afterglow of the splendid Elizabethan sunset, watches his Devon maids bringing in whitethorn on May Day.

After that, the babbling almost ceases; but soon there is a little parson at Selborne writing more sweetly about birds than anyone had ever done before, and through a strange troubled countryside lit by the rick-fires of the Agricultural Revolution William Cobbett rides boisterously, pausing now and then to admire a good crop of swedes. And then there is George Borrow, going gustily about Wales as if he were carried along by the great winds that blow off Glyder Fawr; and then Richard Jefferies, finding new wonders in a dusty hedgerow, and W. H. Hudson, watching the birds and writing about them in such prose as a man might use who had watched the angels.

But the factories were growing up where the grass had grown, and industry was changing the face of England; in the hurry to make money and guns the green fields were almost forgotten, save by Mr Belloc, striding over his Sussex Downs, and by a little group of young poets who, in the hush before the great storm broke over Europe, were rediscovering England almost too late. Within a year or two they were buckling on their uniform to go to the war; but they still babbled of green fields for a little longer, until one by one they died in the mud. . . .

Now that the storm is over, there seem to be fresh storms brewing yet; but the catkins still dance on the hazel-stems in March, and the moths still come to the honeysuckle in June, and the ragged robin blows in the autumn hedge. Horse-hoofs still beat out their old hexameters across the wide grasslands in November; and here and there, in the long summer evenings, men in white flannels play their preposterous lovely game on village greens. A few countrymen still care for these things, and weave tales and write verses about them; but for the most part the tales are a wistful looking-back and the poems are a requiem. Perhaps the brief episode that was English country life is nearly over, and perhaps the men who babbled of green fields will soon be forgotten. That is why I write this little book, before it is too late; lest the future belong to the machines, and the new poets who sing them.

Country Men

HORSES

My Kingdom for a horse

SHAKESPEARE

In his later life, when John and his wife, Lucile, moved to the lovely mill house at Kemerton, close to the foot of Bredon Hill, his mare, Zena, brought him incomparable pleasure. She was an effervescent, unpredictable character, but John understood her temperamental ways and there was a close bond between them, though there *were* occasions when she deftly decanted him, as he described in a letter to me, enclosed in a copy of his latest book, *The Year of the Pigeons*, in October, 1963 . . . 'I doubt if you can get BBC Midlands TV, but in case you can, have a look at me on Zena in a programme called *Six-Ten* on Monday. It is in connexion with the publication of *The Year of the Pigeons*. Unfortunately Zena didn't like the film camera and was terribly naughty, and for my part, as an exhibition of horsemanship the whole thing is bound to be ludicrous! The purpose of the operation was to show me riding Z. over Bredon Hill. But most of the time she was up on end at horrid angles. I didn't come off. But she *did* have me off on the hill on Wednesday. Full gallop, a pheasant got up under her feet. I sped for miles through the air and rolled over 3 times, and was quite unhurt though winded.'

Not long before his death in 1967, he experienced the unutterable joy of watching Zena give birth to the foal for which he had waited with eager expectancy for eleven months. He wrote movingly of this unforgettable small miracle in the pages of the *Birmingham Mail*, for which he produced weekly articles over a period of many years.

When we moved house to the Lower Mill Farm, and for the first time in my life I found myself the owner of a field or two, I set about looking for a horse to put in my fields. I bought myself a thoroughbred bay mare, called Zena: quick and tireless and sensitive and gay. Now all about me lay the countryside which I love best, and know best, in all England. So possessed by the fun of being on a horse's back again, I rode Zena far afield, across my neighbour's barley stubbles which in autumn are like a western prairie right at my back door; up and over our hill with its oakwoods and its springy pastures; through the market-gardens where a score of assorted crops makes a many-coloured hem all round the green skirt of the hill; down the deep lanes, between flowery hedgerows; along the banks of our stream where the mills have clacked since Domesday; over the commons, beside the slow rivers, or far across country to look at the haunts of my boyhood again.

From Zena's back I watched the seasons come and go; I looked over the hedges and saw the crops planted and the crops reaped; and covering so many miles, yet at a pace not too quick for looking at things, I got to know the familiar land in a way I had never known it before. Also, I saw it changing before my eyes, as the new motor-road slashed through it, the suburbs crept out and out from the little towns, immemorial elms came down, the great yellow Cats purred and roared in the old orchards, lumbering to and fro, bunting down the cider-apple trees that no longer served any purpose but to delight the eye. And everywhere I saw how the new techniques of scientific agriculture imposed their new totalitarian order upon the land; so that sometimes, despite much loveliness that is left for a little longer, I would look across country from Zena's back and see, spread out before me, a battlefield in which the tragic conflict between man and nature was being bitterly fought out.

You can see a lot of landscape from horseback, and in the course of a long ride alone you have plenty of time to think, to speculate and to remember. Out of those rides, those thoughts, those speculations and those memories, came the chapters which follow.

The Year of the Pigeons

M y beloved mare Zena gave birth to a chestnut filly foal right on the dot; round about the stroke of midnight on the date she was due.

Birth always seems to me a bit of a miracle, and it seemed all the more so that night as the long-leggity foal lay sprawling in the straw, and Zena turned her charming head to look at it for the very first time; and – before she began to lick it – softly, delightedly, whinnied.

Close to the foal lay the crumpled envelope in which nature delivers such parcels, arranged with care and neatness which cannot fail to touch your heart.

Nosetip close to the two forehoofs, ears laid back, the hindlegs drawn up close beneath the belly.

The whole beautiful present is packed with an eye to convenience and safety of delivery, streamlined, tidy, awesomely well-contrived.

As it happened, the day before my foal was born, I had been reading the latest issue of 'Paris Match.'

It contained a feature captioned *Voici le poulain du premier jour de printemps* – and indeed the photograph, taken at the very moment of birth, showed 'the foal of the first day of spring' lying on a bed of spring flowers, somewhere in Greece.

It was one of the most dramatic, exciting and beautiful photographs I have ever seen.

The grey mare had got up and broken the cord which joined the foal's life to hers.

But the veil, as the French call the envelope, was still attached to her, though the foal, with ears plastered back, struggling forelegs, and wide eyes seeing grass, flowers, sky and mother for the very first time, had partly struggled out of it.

One thought of a parachutist, just come to earth.

'A peine ne,' went on the caption, *'il y a la force de s'arc-bouter sur ses jambes.'* 'Only just born, there is the strength of a flying-buttress in its legs'; and as our foal struggled to get up that vivid phrase came back into my mind.

Its legs were immensely powerful; but it hadn't learned how to co-ordinate them, so that it had to use them separately and individually, as props, little flying-buttresses, to support its body as it tried to stand.

Again the whole business was most touching and tender, and it was all one could do to refrain from interfering.

We opened a bottle of champagne in the loose box at 2 a.m., and drank the health of the foal still struggling in the straw.

It would get to its feet, stagger a little, go down flop.

At long last it achieved a brief stability: all four flying buttresses splayed outwards from the body; and we propped it against our knees while its lips sought the first drink of its young life.

Zena whinnied, turned her head again, licked her filly's still-wet hindquarters.

Then the flying-buttresses gave way and the foal collapsed spread-eagled beneath its mother's belly.

But soon it was up again, breathless, desperate, staggering, ridiculous, held together it seemed only by the inexorable life-force which drives all nature's children to suffer in order to survive.

It didn't even know yet where the milk was to be found; it nuzzled between Zena's forelegs, experienced the first little paddy of its young life when it found that there was nothing to be had there.

But Zena whinnied, soothingly; and at last by trial and error and a bit of luck, the foal's questing mouth found what it was searching for.

Zena's ancestors, which lived in wild herds over the plains of central and eastern Europe, were subject to various predators, some more cunning, some more swift-footed, than they.

The predators included men whose arrows sped faster than the wind, and wolves hungry after the long winter, ravening at the breeding-time of the mares.

Within a few hours of being born, a foal might have to run beside its mother, to keep up with the whole thundering herd. Only the sound and the swift ones survived.

Hence those astonishingly long hindlegs, which so quickly lose their clumsiness.

As I write this the week-old foal keeps pace with its mother as she canters round the paddock.

It moves beautifully, with long easy strides – as indeed it should do, since its grandfather won the Derby.

You will hear a good deal more of it, I daresay, in this column.

Birmingham Mail, 9 June 1967

In *The Waters under the Earth*, his last and most ambitious novel, John achieved some wonderfully descriptive writing and showed rare imaginative powers. In an earlier book, *Midsummer Meadow*, he had revealed something of his almost divine gift when he wrote of 'The young nymph', Hazel, transfixed at the sight of a family of wild otters in a Gloucestershire stream; how 'all her senses and perceptions were projected towards the creatures in the pool; she had long ceased to be a watcher of the dance, she had become a participant. She was *being otter*, she was feeling the cool creamy surge on her own skin, the tang of the bursting bubbles, the hardness of the water and the softness of the air; she was smelling the sweet river-smell, seeing the dark darting underwater shapes and the bright scatter of spray, knowing the frenzy and the fury and the wild delight . . . He understood because he himself before now had so projected himself; he had launched himself into the teeth of a nor' wester with the wild geese in winter, his spirit storm-tossed as their bodies, he had watched a stoat with a rabbit and had been for a split second both hunter and hunted, had known both the cruel triumph and the pain.'

When he came to write *The Waters under the Earth* John exhibited this uncanny talent by entering deeply into the heart and mind of his heroine, and, though the most masculine of men, did so with such insight that he was able to feel and think exactly as a young girl on the threshold of life.

This imaginative streak enlivened all his writings, whether on the subject of the sport and countryside which he loved so well, or the characters which he portrayed so vividly.

Beyond Elmbury the road began to climb towards the hills. Signposts pointed to places with names which were lordlier, lovelier or stranger than those which belonged to the vale: Temple Guiting and Guiting Power, Condicote and Evenlode, Turkdean and Cutsdean, Upper and Lower Slaughter, Upper and Lower Swell . . . 'Getting into the Daglingworth country,' laughed Janet; and over the next rise they came in sight of Stow-on-the-Wold, 'where the Devil caught cold', standing on the summit of its sheep-bitten down. The Devil wouldn't have caught cold there today: out of a sky as empty as the wold the sun blazed down upon the surging, murmurous, whinneying conglomeration of men and horses, on the slope beneath the old stone town.

Stow Fair was an Occasion; nothing remotely like it happened within hundreds of miles. You stepped back centuries when you followed the multitudinous hoofmarks down to that field full of folk. Only the horses were contemporary: the humans all seemed to belong to some other day than ours. There were huge Hogarthian farmers, rolling as they walked, landlubbers who had caught the sailor's gait from their undulating downs. There were shepherds lean as their collies, Landseer-subjects with Landseer-dogs at heel. There were immemorial gipsies bitterly bargaining as they sold each other piebald ponies: the Romany version of taking in each other's washing. There were impoverished gentry, starveling by comparison with those tunbellied yeomen who'd grown fat out of their flocks – the kind of faded, shrunken, mildly eccentric, threadbare, but unmistakable gentry who lived on the crumbs of dividends deriving from the minutest holdings of War Loan, in dilapidated draughty cottages situated at Dead Ends; who kept, perhaps, in a tumbledown orchard a single, sacred, elderly, beloved brood mare, and brought her annual foals to be sold at Stow.

(And when she grew old and barren, Tony fantasticated to Susan, the family would stint themselves to buy her oats and good hay, they would make her linseed mashes every Saturday until she died, when they would dig a deep grave among the broken barren apple trees and bury her with their own hands rather than handle the abhorred knacker's four-pounds-ten!)

Then there were the sharp-nosed, narrow-eyed horse dealers, with tiny fish-like mouths, so that everything they said seemed to be top secret. Fellows like them had hung about the heels of John Mytton, and sold the thoroughbreds which they coarsely called cattle to such breakneck young bucks as Susan's ancestors back in the eighteen-hundreds. Today they stood in the crowd turning wary eyes this way and that, picking out the hunting folk, who indeed were as colourful a lot as you'd find in the pages of Jorrocks, ranging from a hermaphrodite Squarson (half a parson, half a squire) to the fiery General Bouverie M.F.H. who swore most terribly out hunting and whose rich repertory of oaths included such curiosities as 'Fishcakes and Haemorrhoids!'

Lastly there was the usual rout of ragtag-and-bobtail hangers-on who inhabit the fringe of the horse world always, the very spit and image of those you meet with in faded sporting prints of the inferior kind, hung in the snugs and back-bars of old-fashioned countrified hotels: old broken-down grooms, vagabonds from Ireland, warned-off jockeys, bowlegged ex-huntsmen and whips, ex-farmers ruined by racing and booze, who in their cups remembered, as if it were another life, the point-to-points they'd won in the nineteen-thirties. Crippled by long horsemanship, these stable riffraff hobbled to and fro between the two beer tents, leaning on sticks, cursing the arthritis in hip and knee; yet if they could live their lives over again they'd ride just as hard and recklessly, swig their Dutch courage out of the same-shaped bottles, take the same tosses, and break the same bones!

And there were the children, wild as those broken ones had once been, wilder than the Cotswold hares.

The children galloped everywhere. In whatever direction you looked there was a bit of a rodeo going on. Tony and Susan watched two boys holding a long pole between them while a pretty little blonde aged fourteen or so, trying out a new pony, jumped it backwards and forwards, bareback, with only a halter rope to hold on by. Each time she jumped the boys lifted the pole higher. Soon she fell off, the tough little boys yelled with delight, and the pony tore away riderless, scattering the crowd, barging into the slow ones and causing the nervous ones to barge into their neighbours, followed by shouts, guffaws, oaths and cheers wherever it galloped.

Tony protectively took Susan's arm after that, and she, filled with indescribable bliss, squeezed his to her side, greatly surprising him. He remembered her last night, suddenly grown up in the scanty flame-coloured dress, and he let the speculations play idly in his mind. Susan, knowing nothing about them, tossed her head like the young horses, and thought she would have liked to buck and plunge too in accord with their high spirits. Janet stopped to pass the time of day with someone who long ago had sold her a horse or bought one from her, while Tony and Susan wandered on together among the eighteenth-century crowd. In one ring an auctioneer with a voice like a corncrake was selling the hunters. In another an auctioneer who roared like the Bull of Bashan was selling second-hand farm machinery. In yet a third a young clerk with a chirp as penetrating and persistent as a chiff-chaff's was selling harness and stable sundries – Here's a job lot for you, ladies and gents, halter and two headropes, martingale, haynet, lungeing-rein, canvas stable bucket, old horse-rug has the moth in it but still serviceable, one pound fifteen shillings, thank you, sir, two pounds I'm bid, going at forty shillings . . .

Horses everywhere, browns, bays, chestnuts, dapples, duns, palominos, skewbalds, strawberry roans, fleabitten greys, one albino with vacant pale china-blue eyes, 17-hand hunters, chunky cobs, broken-down hacks, children's ponies podgy from grass, argybargy young colts, fat mares with spindle-legged foals, screamed, neighed, whinneyed, said Ha! ha!, stamped, kicked, bit, reared. All round there was bustle and bargaining, chipping, cheating, cozening, shouting, swearing; rough fun, broad comedy, grotesquerie, sheer savagery. The cruelties made Susan wince. A man who wasn't a gipsy but looked gipsyish pointlessly slashed with a heavy whip a Shetland pony no bigger than a dog. An oaf with a suffused and bloated face, running along with a young horse to show his paces to a possible buyer, gave him a cunning back-handed flip with a cane under his belly, deliberately aimed at his genitals, with the idea of making him step out. Susan *became horse* for a horrible second, writhed in *her* belly, felt the cut between *her* legs. She cried out and tugged at Tony's arm. She wanted him to perform some large dramatic act of chivalry: stride nobly forward, knock the brute down . . . But Tony, if he noticed it at all, accepted the incident as part of the pattern, something inherent in the rough tough scene, which was rather like a Breughel canvas – sometimes you saw it whole, a teeming microcosm of life, at others some trifling detail held your eye and you found yourself dwelling on it willy-nilly. Into his vision now came galumphing a tubby roan mare whose owner had no doubt represented her as being faster and more spirited – even perhaps more dangerous to life and limb – than she had ever been in her long-lost youth. But the moment of truth had now arrived, the owner had been challenged by the prospective buyer to get up on her back, and however hard he dug his heels into her well-covered ribs she lolloped along leisurely, pursued by mocking cries:

'Light her up for me, then, set her alight!'

The phrase made a kind of poetry in Tony's ears, and as he turned with a grin to Susan she nodded in quick appreciation, he didn't have to explain why that '*Set her alight!*' had stirred his spirit. Suddenly they were as close as they'd been when they went birdsnesting and climbing together in the woods at Doddington.

Janet rejoined them, and they looked for a quiet spot where they might eat their sandwiches without the risk of being trampled to death. Tony thought he saw an open space against the railings, at the far corner of the field; so they made their way towards it.

'Oh, look!' cried Susan suddenly; and they all three stopped and stared.

The ribby, rakish, dangerous-looking mare had four white fetlocks, perfectly matching. For the rest she was jet-black all over from nose to tail. Probably the open space which Tony had noticed was one she had cleared for herself by her antics; there wasn't another horse within thirty yards. Now she stood stock-still, but with a dramatic stillness, and the pale-faced weaselly man who was in charge of her stood stock-still at her head, and both of them looked as if they were aware of a time-bomb's ticking and had been frozen into stillness as they waited for the bang.

'Four white socks,' said Tony. 'Isn't there a rhyme?'

'One, buy; two, try; three, shy; four, fly!' Janet said. 'It's supposed to be unlucky if a horse has four.' She was turning over the pages of her catalogue. 'Here she is. "Lot 11. Black mare 5 years, 15.3, sound in wind and limb. A spectacular performer". I bet she is! Her name's Nightshade, by the way.'

Susan remembered the wicked fruit she had found once when she was a child, by a damp ditchside at Doddington. She'd perilously nibbled one before Janet cried 'Deadly nightshade!' and took it from her. Glossy as that berry was the black mare's coat in the sun. When she moved the light and shade in quick alternation ran along the muscles which Leonardo loved to draw, little flickering impulses ran down her shoulder or rippled along her flank, like catspaws upon a shimmering sea.

Meanwhile Tony, who loved to pretend he was a likely customer for a horse so that he might enjoy the lies which its owner told about it, had detached himself from Susan and was talking to the furtive-looking fellow who held the black mare's bridle, but who eyed her as warily as if she had been a Black Widow spider poised to strike. He whispered to Tony from beneath his little whiskery moustache, so Susan and Janet could only catch a sentence now and then, when hyperbole took hold of him and discretion was thrown to the winds. Oh, she was a flying machine! She'd lep a haystack, lep a house, lep the course at Aintree with her legs tied together. The word 'active' recurred several times. Apparently she was somewhat too 'active' for the chicken-hearted folk one met nowadays. She'd given evidence of this activity in the ring when she came under the hammer; so nobody would bid her price and she'd been withdrawn from sale. Weasel would send her to the knacker's, and then cut his own throat, rather than accept the miserable sum he had been offered.

Janet nudged Susan's arm. Tony had noticed some fault or blemish, and he took a step nearer to the black mare. Yes, there was a long jagged scar running down the off-hind from stifle joint to hock. Tony bent down to have a look, and as he did so the mare nervously swung round and turned her hindquarters towards the sun, which showed up some smaller scars on her near hind leg as well. Tony, having spotted the injuries, pressed his advantage to the full. 'Accident in traffic?' he inquired casually, but in a tone which suggested all sorts of dark suspicions: that the mare would shy at every motor-bike and bolt a mile if she met a bus. Weasel raised his voice in passionate denial; he waved his free arm too, and this so alarmed the mare that she went back on her hocks, heaving him towards her by the reins. It seemed to Susan, as she watched the little drama, that at last the truth was being dragged out of him, painfully and against his will, as he braced himself against the mare's tugging, and the admissions came from between his teeth in little breathless gasps.

Traffic? She wouldn't turn her head to look at the Lord Mayor's Show. Wouldn't take no notice of a regiment of tanks.

It was in the show ring, mister.

We tried to make her into a jumper. She'd clear a five-barred gate as if it was no more trouble than steppin' over a thripenny-bit in the roadway.

But she hadn't got the temperament for it: hotted up in the ring.

My kid brother was on her back. Suddenly she was bilin' over and leppin' into the elements.

Over the ropes as if she was flyin' Becher's.

Into the car park, kickin' spots off the cars. And my kid brother took to horspital.

Tore the skin off her legs, but I got a vet's certificate, here it is, mister, sound in wind *and* limb.

If anyone wanted her for a show jumper I'd shoot her, mister, I'd shoot *meself*, rather than sell her to him.

But if a young gent like yourself, who I can see by the look of you *likes* 'em a bit active, wanted a good-lookin' young hunter that'd lep a haystack –

Tony at this point began to run his hand down the mare's near fetlock. She put her ears back and edged away. Susan could hear Weasel swearing at her under his breath, and she thought how the vicious small sound would frighten you if you were an animal in his power. Then suddenly she noticed something extraordinary. Over the mare's glossy neck a dark matt patch was slowly spreading; wet streaks from it seeped down her shoulders. Tony had spotted it now, and was staring at it in surprise. He laid his hand on the sweating shoulder, gave Weasel a look, wiped his hand ostentatiously on a handkerchief, and came back to Janet and Susan.

'What do you make of that, Cousin Janet?' he asked.

'At some time or other, she's been beaten up.'

'She might have been quite something,' Tony said, glancing back at her. 'She's perfectly sound as far as I can tell.'

'Well, they've certainly ruined her now. There's big money in show jumpers, so I suppose you get these fools on the fringe of the business who imagine you can make a horse jump by frightening it to death.'

The mare still twitched and trembled. Raw with pity Susan went up to her. Tony and Janet watched as she put her hand on the high withers, stretched out her fingers and began to tease out the long mane. The ears, that had been laid right back like a squatting rabbit's, began to flex forward at last.

'Goodness, look at that!' Tony said.

Janet smiled. 'Seems it's men she's frightened of.'

The sweat-patches still showed like charcoal smudges against the shine, but the panic which engendered them was dying down. The twitching and quivering ceased. Susan, looking pleased with herself, cocked an eye at the saddle, as if to say 'Shall I?' Tony recognised that look – Susan at the age of nine or so looking up the trunk of a just-climbable tree: Shall I, shan't I, yes I must! For some reason the recognition delighted him; and now she turned her head and gave him a grin, inviting a dare. 'May she?' he said to Janet, who laughed; 'She can look after herself.' The aunt, Ferdo's sister, whom Susan had stayed with during the war, was one of the wilder Seldons; she went in for young Irish horses, straight from the bog. Susan had spent most of her holidays on and off their backs from the age of seven until she was twelve.

'Up you get, then!' Tony called.

Weasel, whose pinched face and tremulous moustache reflected all his emotions, turned from Susan to Tony in dismay; he had few principles, but murder was not in his commission, the look seemed to say. At last he offered the reins to Susan as reluctantly as if he were the apothecary of Mantua handing the poison to Romeo. He then retreated rapidly, muttering 'Mind you, she's active' in admonition or excuse. Tony went forward to give Susan a hand. She'd collected up the reins, and already the mare was beginning to dance. 'Matthew, Mark, Luke and John, Hold my horse while I get on!' she laughed, pleasing him again with a reminder of their childhood, when she used to say the rhyme. He caught hold of the reins and stood by the mare's head.

'Want a leg up?'

'No, I'll jump. Hang on.' Then she was in the saddle crying 'I've got her,' was feeling for the stirrups, had gathered the reins. Weasel's moustache twitched and 'his nose was as sharp as a pen' as he gazed up at Susan, casual and collected in her old blue jeans, which she'd nearly grown out of and were rucked up to her knees.

The mare stood still; but it was a dynamic stillness. Susan was conscious of a sort of suppressed panic *rippling* as it were underneath her seat. It struck her for the first time that this fairground must appear to Nightshade just as alarming as the show ring from which she had incontinently bolted. The crowd made a pattern of continual menace as it surged this way and that, converged, scattered, receded, advanced, and performed small purposeless antics like a hive of disturbed ants. Now from one quarter, now from another, rose raucous inexplicable sounds. Yahoos! thought Susan, getting a Houyhnhnm's eye view of them.

Sitting there, patting Nightshade's neck, altogether possessed by compassion for the wild misused thing, she didn't hear the thudding hoofs until they were almost upon her, until Tony was raising an arm in warning and Nightshade like a rocket was going up in the air. Then Susan heard the thuds, looked over her shoulder, and saw the peaceable galumphing roan, prodded at last into some semblance of activity, coming full tilt at Nightshade from the rear. The owner, himself alarmed by his unaccustomed speed, was shouting 'Out of my way!' while the prospective buyer continued to utter his strange poetic abracadabra, *Light her up for me, set her alight!* as he raced along with wildly flapping arms, like a plump bustard inadequately winged that tries in vain to get up enough speed for a take-off.

Susan felt Nightshade rising up between her thighs, and thought: She's going to bolt and nothing I can do will stop her. She'd never been afraid on a horse before; now for a moment she had the same odd feeling of purely physical fear which she had when she climbed to the top of Elmbury Abbey tower and dared herself to lean over the parapet and look down. The feeling had been right down in her stomach, almost sexy. It was uncomfortable but there had been a temptation to tease herself with it, to look over the parapet again and again.

For two or three seconds, now, Susan's body knew this extraordinary fear-feeling that lay half-way between pleasure and pain. During that brief space the roan passed within feet of her, Nightshade's sideways leap sent Weasel scurrying, and the mare got her head down, so that there was nothing in front of Susan at all. For a moment it was touch and go. Then, feeling her mouth as she shortened the reins, Susan collected her together, imposed her authority, took command, and turned her in a wide circle, cantering delightfully on the razor edge of fear.

She came back to Janet, and pulled up so gently that Nightshade, shortening the pace of her canter, seemed to be doing a series of small diminishing bucks without moving forward, an agreeable rocking-horse motion which made Janet laugh.

'We didn't expect to see you back for quite a long time,' Janet said.

Tony was confabulating with Weasel. They both looked very earnest. Susan heard the word 'guineas' and thought Tony was amusing himself at Weasel's expense, by pretending that he was going to buy.

Forty guineas a leg then, said Weasel, and it's givin' her away. His morale had been boosted by Susan's safe return. You saw how a slip of a girl could handle her, he cried gleefully. I'll be lookin' for a hook to hang meself on, if I part with her for less then forty guineas a leg.

Some mysterious taboo, such as primitive tribes have, forbade him at this stage to state his price in so many words. Tony, bargaining for the fun of it, fell in with the convention and remarked pleasantly that considering the animal's history anybody who offered more than twenty-five guineas a leg would want his head looking at. Weasel edged closer, and putting his tiny mouth within inches of Tony's ear, hissed passionately: *Thirty-five guineas a leg and for God's sake don't say yes or I'll be shootin' meself tomorrow!*

Tony thought that if he were a horse-dealer he would always put up a pretty girl on any animal he was trying to sell. Susan, flushed and excited, her hair all over the place, tossing back her head, added fifty pounds to Nightshade's value.

Suddenly the idea came into his mind: Well, why *not* buy her the mare, now she's so beautifully shown us how to ride her? He could well afford it: he'd had a good bet last week, nine to four in tenners. Rather fun to give Susan a little surprise. He was still puzzled, surprised, amused and a little bit excited, by her growing-up.

He whispered to Weasel, whose secretive ways seemed to be catching: I'll bid you a hundred guineas, take it or leave it.

A hundred and thirty, Weasel whispered back.

Not on your life, a hundred and ten.

Look here, Guv'nor, breathed Weasel, make it a hundred and twenty-five, and I'll give you back a fiver for luck.

At the mere prospect of his having to do so, a sort of sacrificial spasm shook his meagre frame. Shake hands on it, Guv', he wheezed in agony, shake hands before I changes me mind!

Susan didn't understand what it was about. How unpleasant for Tony to be shaking hands with Weasel!

She was still on Nightshade's back, determined to remain there until the last moment, appalled at the prospect of handing her back into Weasel's charge. Love and pity tore at her, for she could still sense the ripples of suppressed panic going on under the saddle, and she knew that she was still personally engaged with that panic, as she tried to send messages of encouragement along the reins. She knew that if she relaxed for a moment, and some small untoward occurrence took her unawares, Nightshade would be off again, madly bolting away from some invisible inaudible Terror galloping at her heels. It was lovely to feel that she held the whole spirit of the mare in her two hands. She hummed to herself, because she was still happily afraid.

Tony with a final nod to Weasel came back to them.

'What on earth have you been up to?' Janet asked him.

'You don't really mind, Cousin Janet, do you?' He always used that old-fashioned style, Cousin Ferdo, Cousin Janet, taking pleasure in the quaint formality yet half-mocking at it. He had a way, which Susan loved, of affecting rather elaborate manners, kissing your hand or helping you out of a car with an air, while at the same time he seemed to be laughing at himself for his affectation. 'Dear Cousin Janet, *please* don't be cross. But Susan rides her so beautifully; it suddenly struck me that she might make something of her – something really good: and after all, her birthday's not very far off.'

The Waters under the Earth

I've got a curious mind in both senses: it always seeks to know the why and the wherefore, and it sometimes troubles itself with matters so foolish and trivial that nobody in his wits would think about them at all. For instance, riding over the hill today I began puzzling my head about Zena's flies. In close summer weather the flies always distress her, and I thought it might be a welcome relief to her when I saddled up and rode her to the top of Bredon. But of course there were flies there too. She tossed her head and flexed her ears, trying to shake them off. I began to observe these flies.

They were the same sort as those which tormented her in the paddock: that is to say they were about the same size as house-flies and they belonged to the species called *Hydrotaea irritans*. This kind of fly does not bite or sting; but it is attracted to small wounds and sores on the bodies of animals – especially to the mucus secretions of the eyes and nostrils. It also delights in human sweat, as campers in hot weather quickly discover. It settles on the forehead or the neck and actually drinks the sweat, causing a horrible tickling with its legs and mouth parts. In my paddock during the hours of daylight Zena always has about a score of these flies buzzing around her head. And there's no escape from them, for wherever the mare goes, her attendant flies follow.

Now the idea began to occur to me that the flies which tormented Zena on Bredon Hill were perhaps *the same individuals* which teased her in the paddock; and I began to watch the flies very carefully, to see if in fact they were following us as we went along or if the fly population was continually changing. But it was very difficult to tell (*Time flies we cannot they fly so fast!* as the schoolboys' catch-phrase goes). I kept my eyes on a single fly for about ten minutes. For much of this time it sat on Zena's neck; but every now and then it took wing and buzzed about her right ear, which she flicked angrily. Now, I thought, let's trot and see if we can leave it behind. It kept station, still orbiting the ear. Very well; we'll play a trick on it, I thought. I dug my heels into Zena's sides suddenly. If you're acquainted with what John Masefield, in *Reynard the Fox*, so nicely described as

> *The high quick gingery ways of thoroughbreds*

you can imagine Zena's response. She gave one great bound, and was off. I no longer, of course, was able to keep observation on *Hydrotaea irritans*. Zena gathered pace and went along with splendid strides. The sheep-cropped turf was soft under her hoofs. I had to hold her tight, because if she ever gets her head right down it's a job to stop her. At any rate, I thought, as the most exhilarating wind whistled by and I shed quite a lot of years for just a few seconds, We've left those damned flies behind!

Not a bit of it. The very moment I pulled her up the flies were about Zena's head again. Of course I can't swear they were the identical ones. *Hydrotaea irritans*, whose larva feed in cowpats, is abundant almost everywhere you go. But we were in the middle of an open down, and it seems unlikely, to say the least, that a score or so specimens of *Hydrotaea irritans* were lying in readiness, at the very spot where we stopped, to buzz about the streak of mucus which Zena, breathing hard, blew down her nostrils. I feel sure, therefore, that they were 'our flies', the same ones we set out with. Then did they fly along beside us, at some 28 m.p.h.? Or did they cling on to Zena's head, desperately keeping their grip, during her mad career? I see them behaving like gulls in a gale, which follow their own ship, continually circling it, and now and then, for a brief rest, settle upon her rigging.

The Year of the Pigeons

N ext morning Ralph rode the chestnut to sell.
He possessed that virtue which is the gift of the gods – *hands*. He was both gentle and firm with a horse's mouth; but there was something more than that, a trick of quieting a fretting horse by the reins alone, which one can neither describe nor explain. When the gods give, they give generously.

Hussar, good-mannered in other respects, had a habit of tossing his head in a canter, bucking suddenly, and then tearing away with his head down and the bit between his teeth. So long as you kept his head up you were safe enough; but if ever he managed to get away with you, the sooner you fell off the luckier you might consider yourself.

Ralph's difficulty this morning was to keep his horse's head up and at the same time prevent him from tossing it about and seeming to fret at the bit. The showing-off of Hussar required something more than skill – an artistry.

And how he hated it! The constant watchfulness for a likely buyer, whereas he should have been watchful for hounds and foxes; the staid canters to and fro; the enforced cautiousness – one must not take an undue risk lest Hussar came down; the subtle meanness of the whole business. Besides, Hussar had carried him well for a couple of seasons; he was fond of the horse. Now he supposed he would have to rely upon borrowing; and a lent horse is never the same as one of your own.

Hounds finished about two o'clock. They had let a cub bolt from the larch covert and rattled him nicely over a mile or two to Brackenbury Scrub, where they marked him to ground and left him. Dixon missed Ralph among the horsemen at the finish; he waited for a few minutes, and then rode home alone.

Ralph came back about tea-time, and found Dixon in the stables bandaging a swollen fetlock.

'Well, dad, I've sold Hussar.'

Dixon looked up quickly. 'Sold him? How much?'

'Seventy. Ten pounds more than you asked. It was a bit of luck; a man from the Cotswold country. He wants him boxed at Brackenbury tomorrow.'

Dixon was a person of few words. To Ralph the man he said: 'Well done! We'll go shares in Judy.'

Dixon's Cubs

Oh, the sizzling, the stamping, the hot-iron smells and the burnt-hoof smells, the sparks that flew like little shooting-stars, in the dim-dark smithy in the days of my youth! Next to the taxidermist's shop in the neighbouring town, where there were stuffed owls and otters, boxes of glass eyes, tropical butterflies, fearful scalpels and strong whiffs of naphthalene, the blacksmith's was the most exciting establishment I knew. Everybody is romantic about blacksmiths: there's Longfellow's hackneyed poem, and Gerard Manley Hopkins' grand one – he wrote it, you'll remember, to a farrier who'd lost his strength, and pined, and sickened, and died –

> *Poor Felix Randal,*
> *How far from then forethought of, all thy more boisterous years,*
> *When thou at the random grim forge, powerful amidst peers,*
> *Didst fettle for the great grey drayhorse his bright and battering sandal!*

The blacksmith who caught my imagination when I was a child was called, not very appositely, Mr White. He shod, not only hunters, but the drayhorses of the Midland Railway and the shaggy-fetlocked Shire horses and the huge Suffolk Punches that drew the farm-wagons at haytime and harvest and ploughed the fields in winter, heaving hoofs bigger than dinner plates step by step with the sticky soil upon them, as they plodded their eight miles of hard-going in the course of a seven-hour day to plough three roods of ground with a nine inch furrow.

In my memory they are splendid and stupid, patient most of the time but liable to sudden panics, not knowing their own strength. Mr White's muscles really did stand out like iron bands when he lifted their hind hoofs, gripped them between his knees, hammered in the nails to secure the 'bright and battering sandal'.

When I was old enough to have a hunter I took it to be shod by Mr White and got to know him well enough to have some long talks while the job was done. He claimed that as a Sergeant Farrier in the Boer War he'd shod for Winston Churchill the horse on which he escaped from his brief captivity by the Boers. But Mr White was gloomy about the prospects for his trade:

'I be the last on 'em. There wun't be any more, hereabouts. The world's changing, and they've no use for we any more.'

He was utterly mistaken. The Suffolk Punches and the great grey drayhorses have disappeared; but there are still the hunters – at least as many as there were in 1939 – the flourishing pony clubs with their innumerable fat Thelwell ponies and their countless pony-mad Thelwell schoolgirls, there are pony-trekkers in the hill-country, then at the riding schools and of course the point-to-points, the training stables and the races still.

In fact, I daresay there are *more* horses, within say a 20-mile radius of my house, than there were in the late Thirties. The social levelling-down and levelling-up has meant, as it was bound to do, that more and more people can afford ponies for their children. And why not? This seems to me the most agreeable aspect of socialism; that more people can afford the sort of fun which I, as a moderately 'privileged' country boy, enjoyed in my childhood. Likewise, more adults can afford to go to riding-schools, take part in pony-treks, even to hunt foxes. Only people with chips on their shoulders can object to this. Meanwhile the blacksmith, whose job is now diversified by the demand for quick repair of farm machinery and for the manufacture of arty wrought-ironwork for newcomers to the countryside, is more in demand than ever he was before. Few of us, nowadays, take our horses to his forge; he shoes them as I learned to do myself years and years ago when I was a Territorial soldier, by cold shoeing. He comes along with his assistant in a small van and brings with him some suitable shoes for the particular horses we've asked him to shoe that day. He keeps in his mind, as all blacksmiths should, a clear picture of the *feet* of his regular customers. Especially he remembers if there's anything unusual: a slight malformation, a tendency to over-reach, a foot which needs building up a little with an extra-thick shoe. So when we ring up and say 'Zena needs two hind shoes, Skipper wants shoeing all round, Nou-Nou's O.K. except for her near-fore,' he either takes the necessary shoes from his stock or makes them specially in his forge and brings them with him on whichever day of the week he visits our neighbourhood. Then he trims and pares the hoofs and fits the shoes as accurately, I'm sure, as Felix Randal did in his 'random grim forge' where the hoofs sizzled and the sharp smoke from it tickled everybody's noses and the bellows blew and the furnace blazed and the sparks flew like shooting-stars.

Birmingham Mail, 24 March 1967

CONSERVATION

*When you destroy a blade of grass
You poison England at her roots . . .*

GORDON BOTTOMLEY

John was years ahead of his time where conservation was concerned. In his first book ever to be published – *Dixon' Cubs* in 1930, when he was only 23 – he uses as a preface a poem by Gordon Bottomley (*Poems of Thirty Years*, published by Messrs Constable and Co.) in which the future of the English countryside due to man's inhumanity is uncannily forecast.

> *When you destroy a blade of grass*
>   *You poison England at her roots;*
> *Remember no man's foot can pass*
>   *Where evermore no green life shoots.*
>
> *You force the birds to wing too high*
>   *Where your unnatural vapours creep;*
> *Surely the living rocks shall die*
>   *Where birds no rightful distance keep.*
>
> *You have brought down the firmament*
>   *And yet no heaven is more near;*
> *You shape huge deeds without event,*
>   *And half made men believe and fear.*
>
> *Your worship is your furnaces,*
>   *Which, like old idols, lost obscenes,*
> *Have molten bowels; your vision is*
>   *Machines for making more machines.*

Though this poem was addressed 'To Ironfounders and Others' it was an early presage of what was to come; the lethal sprays, the pesticides, all the other horrors perpetrated in the name of progress today.

Dixon's Cubs contained some unusually imaginative and sensitive writing for a young man in his early twenties. In addition to his awareness of the dangers threatening the English countryside, he wrote of the horrors of war as though he had indeed been involved – though the Great War began when he was only six years old. I can recall the astonishment of a friend of mine, meeting John for the first time. *Dixon's Cubs* was what he described as his 'bed-side book' and he had expected to find its author a middle-aged man with first-hand experience of the battlefield. Even at the age of 23 (when the book was published) John possessed an astonishingly mature mental outlook as well as being something of a dreamer, and this novel foreshadowed what was to come in his later literary works.

When he was a small boy we nicknamed him 'Johnny-head-in-air' after the character in that grim book for children – popular at the time – *Strüwwelpeter*, and in many respects the 'Cub' in the novel whom he called 'John' resembled the author; in his youth dreamy, poetic, sensitive, though I do not imagine for a moment that he was in any way consciously attempting a self-portrait, since he was not given to self-analysis.

He was, all his adult life, a fervent conservationist, and he campaigned untiringly during the 1950s and '60s to abolish the senseless and unnecessary spraying of roadside verges. It was due, I believe, largely to his efforts that this practice was eventually discontinued in his native Gloucestershire.

I doubt if you would recognise the Ridge now, for its tameless hunchback shows up badly under the new cottages; but it is still a point of vantage on which to stand and look down the beautiful valley on a fine day. Americans come there, and gasp and catch their breath and murmur to themselves ecstatically, 'So this is England!' But I, for my part, look back towards Brackenbury, and see the smoke of the chimneys and the rusty-red roofs of the suburbs creeping on like some Juggernaut; and of Brockeridge I think, 'So this *was* England!' Then I shudder a little and go down by the new road.

This is a story of the England that is nearly vanished; for the towns creep out and out, and one by one the old country-folk die, and those that remain love the countryside so much that unwittingly they help to kill it by building houses in their favourite spots. Yet perhaps its ancient spirit lives still, and stirs and wonders beneath houses and factories – stirs in small unnoticed weeds and in stunted bushes and in the strong, rich soil; for this is the England that is older than its oldest cities.

Brockeridge Farm, where the Dixons lived, drew its sustenance from the light brick-coloured loam which overlies the old red sandstone. It stood in the middle of a county of little hills, so green, so round, and so plentiful that they reminded one of monstrous haycocks; silver Wye wound past it and through it on the eastern side; long-horned, white-faced cattle grazed over its fields; and from the meadows at the top of the Ridge one could see the sun go down over the magic mysterious mountains which guard the borders of Wales.

The farm-house was built well and bravely out of hewn blocks of the red sandstone; though now it is surrounded by hideous pink villas under some new housing scheme, since this generation has not the patience nor the muscle to try conclusions with the rock. At the time when this narrative commences, the badgers which gave the place its name still lumbered about round their earths upon the Ridge; and there stood a larch-covert, which harboured regularly two litters of foxes, where the wide tarmac road now runs over the hill. England needed the larches for pit-props in the shortage during the War; and afterwards the bare patch of tree-stumps came in the direct path of the new by-pass road which led from the West Country into South Wales. Thus did circumstances serve the needs of progress, which was very satisfactory for everybody; except perhaps for the foxes, and for a few old-fashioned people who took pleasure in hunting them.

The larch-covert, before the axe came to it, stood upon a hill opposite the farm-house, and when the sun sank down behind it you could see those straight poles catch fire from the sunset. Flecker must have had just such a wood in mind when he wrote of:

> *The olden golden glow of pine-trees,*

and made an immortal line out of the miracle of light.

Prologue to Dixon's Cubs

Just as the Cubs were changing, so was the countryside altering with the times, though more slowly and less noticeably. There was a red pillar-box half-way to Brackenbury. The man in the post office had said: 'It'll be a convenience to you, Mr Dixon.'

'Damn new-fangled idea! . . . Convenience? Why, man, it's an eyesore. My father didn't have a pillar-box, nor my grandfather, and I don't write any more letters than they did. More to do than scribble.'

And indeed it was said that the longest letter Dixon had ever written was that in which he proposed to his wife; and that had consisted of three lines:

Dearest Nan,
    You know I love you. Will you marry me and come to Brockeridge?
                                                         Joseph.

Poor Nan! She was a dear, sad memory now, and it hurt Dixon a little to think of her. She had read between the lines of that brief scrawl – understanding woman that she was – and left a town which she loved and in which she was loved, for the wind-swept loneliness of Brockeridge and the silent unfriendliness of the countryside. It said something for Joseph Dixon that she had never regretted it. He was better with his heart than with his brain; happier with the reins in his hand than with a fountain-pen.

To John, however, the pillar-box was in the nature of a blessing. Often he would slip out and post a letter in it. This new generation was different from the last. England had changed indeed! Here was a Dixon to whom ink was more than the blood of foxes, the pen more than the feel of a horse's mouth!

There were other innovations. One could see the telephone-wires now stretching across the country from Brackenbury to Captain O'Neill's.
 'All the partridges will fly into them,' snorted Dixon.
 'He must be mad.'
 And before the winter had begun, men had started to tarmacadamize the road from Brockeridge to Brackenbury. Motors were becoming more numerous, the county council had pointed out; something must be done for them.
 Driving in to Christmas market, Dixon's chestnut slipped up and broke its knees. 'Damnable!' said Dixon. 'The road's a disgrace to England.'
 It was the beginning of the end.

Dixon's Cubs

Last year our small but enterprising local Naturalists' Society decided to conduct on its own a careful and scientific investigation into the effect of the weed-killer which is sprayed upon the roadside verges to keep them 'tidy' and to save the wages of the roadmen. It obtained the consent of the County Council and with the aid of expert botanists made accurate counts of the plant-population upon two stretches of roadside before and after spraying. Its first report simply blows the technologists' arguments to ribbons. We had anticipated that great damage would be done to the more delicate, beautiful and desirable plants, – especially to the rarest ones which, of course, have a precarious and localized existence anyhow. This apprehension is borne out by the investigation. Such pretty and harmless flowers as the Meadow Vetchling and the Creeping Jenny were completely eliminated by the 'experts' with all the resources of modern science at their command. In all 50% of the desirable species were seriously affected. *But* of the harmful weeds only 30% were reduced in number and only 15% were eliminated! In some cases even those weeds which were affected recovered sufficiently to be able to seed. In short, the wonderful resources of modern science, while able to ruin the beauty of our roadsides, were quite inefficient at doing the job they were meant to do, – so utilitarianism loses even its last mean justification, that it is 'useful'.

Furthermore, the weed-killer destroyed the few hedgerow plants which, apart from their beauty, are actually beneficial. The wild white clover, a valuable source of nectar for bees, – the hedge parsley, and the hogweed, which are important food plants of insects which prey on pests, were seriously damaged. The natural balance was indeed upset; and if the spraying were done on a still larger scale (a mere 800 miles of Gloucestershire roadside were sprayed last year) it is possible that the effect upon farm-crops would be serious.

But perhaps the most alarming part of this report is its last paragraph. The chemists have always insisted, and the users of the spray have dutifully echoed them, that in general the weed-killer was 'selective', i.e. it affected broad-leaved plants more than narrow-leaved ones, and hairy-leaved plants more than smooth ones. But the report states 'It is obvious that there cannot be any rule about this . . . The conclusion is that each plant has for some reason unknown its personal taste or distaste for the spray and no prediction of effect is possible from its physical characteristics.' In other words the stuff is 'selective' only in a random way: *and we don't know what we are doing* when we use it.

The moral of all this seems to be that we should employ the resources of modern science a bit more carefully in future; that we should hesitate to accept the opinions of 'experts' until we have confirmed them by impartial experiment; and that above all we should never allow the technologists to perform their clever little conjuring-tricks without supervision. They are very useful as servants of the community, but we should not allow them to become our masters, for despite their scientific skill they are no more qualified to decide when and where to employ their techniques than a hangman is qualified to judge who shall be hanged. By all means let these 20th-century alchemists make their 20th-century poison, so long as *we* have the last word about the use of them. And by 'we' I mean those of us who are sufficiently civilized to realize that utility is not the sole criterion of judgment; that beauty has an imponderable value; and that you cannot measure the importance of beauty in pounds, shillings and pence.

The Season of the Year

Up on the thistly rough ground at the top of the hill, I was realizing for the first time how much scarcer even our common butterflies are becoming every year. Only a few years ago, in August, it was as if some new exotic flower was growing on the hilltop, a plant that had thistly leaves but variegated white and red and black and orange-tawny florets; and when you came close all these bright flower-heads would take wing and fly away!

But the butterflies are disappearing from the thistle-heads and from the hedgerows; from the railway embankments and from the gardens, where on a buddleia bush at this season you would have seen, only a few summers back, an assortment of red admirals, tortoiseshells, painted ladies, peacocks and commas – with perhaps a yellow brimstone or two for contrast!

The main reason, I dare say, is the destruction of their food-plants: good farming demands that we should get rid of the nettles and thistles upon which many of the caterpillars feed. That can't be helped; but in many places, as I pointed out before, we spray the roadside verges too, pointlessly, wastefully and wantonly. The caterpillars die as the plants blacken and decay; or the eggs hatch when the plant on which they were laid is already dead, the young larvae crawl for a short while on the withered foliage and starve.

Nor do the woodland species escape. Recently the Forestry Commission has begun to employ brushwood killers (powerful hormones in a diesel oil base) to destroy all the undergrowth and small standing trees in preparation for replanting, generally with conifers. The dead trees are left to give shelter to the seedlings. If this practice becomes general it will probably mean the end in Britain of many of our loveliest butterflies, the purple emperor, the white admiral, the silver-washed fritillary.

Does it matter if we lose them? I humbly suggest that it does. Most naturalists are not obscurantist fuddy-duddies; we know the facts about agricultural and sylvan economics. We know that we have got to look at nature in the context of man's ruthless and competitive world. But we are bound to disagree with the utilitarians who see the whole problem as a simple question of money, productivity, balance-sheet profit and loss. We maintain that you cannot really draw up such a balance-sheet because you don't know what this or that butterfly, or butterflies in general, or the roadside wild flowers, or any delight to the eye, may actually be 'worth'. Beauty has an imponderable value, and if we fail to recognize this we are becoming barbarians. After all, nobody suggests that we should build a cathedral in the form of a concrete box because it is cheaper to do so; why then should we assume that it is proper to destroy most of our unique and beautiful deciduous woodlands simply because it is a little more profitable to grow conifers? And looked at in this light, is it *really* airy-fairy poetic nonsense to suggest that there may be some value in an orange-tip or a red admiral butterfly, a value which ought to be set in the balance against a given economic gain?

Nor is it quite certain that the tactics of the utilitarian scientists *do* result in an economic gain. Miss Rachel Carson, in her book *Silent Spring*, suggests that the chemists into whose hands we have delivered the fate of nature, and incidentally of ourselves, simply don't know what they are doing, from the long-term point of view. The incidental killing off of large numbers of agreeable birds, beasts, butterflies, bees, might, I suppose, be acceptable as part of the price we must pay for the privilege of having cheap food. But the horrid truth is beginning to dawn upon even the chemists that *the sprays aren't working effectively any longer; very soon they probably won't work at all; and if so then it is look out for mankind!*

The adaptable insects are becoming resistant to the sprays. Any biologist could have told the chemists that this would happen in the end. House-flies, mosquitoes, ticks and lice all over the world have begun to get accustomed to our chemicals, and indeed on occasions to thrive on them. Flies in the Tennessee valley quickly got used to half a dozen insecticides, including some dangerous organic phosphates employed as a last resort. Cotton pests in the southern United States and in the Sudan are already immune to most of the poisons in the agricultural chemist's appalling repertory. There have also been cases where a particular spray, while killing one pest, has let loose a whole Pandora's box of horrors in the form of new pests which have never before been troublesome, but which have multiplied because their natural enemies have been destroyed.

The implications are hideous. Biologists know – chemists don't – that populations of creatures are kept in check by what they call the resistance of the environment: that is to say, they are controlled by such factors as their natural enemies, the incidence of endemic disease, climatic conditions, and shortage of food. If the resistance breaks down at any point we get a population explosion. Our sprays, because they kill off the natural enemies of *our* enemies, leave the way open for a population explosion on an enormous scale. Insects mostly have many generations a year; their ability to multiply themselves is stupendous; for example Thomas Huxley calculated that a certain female aphis in a single year could produce progeny whose total weight would equal that of all the inhabitants of China!

It is not entirely out of the question that despite man's ingenuity the insects might beat us in the end. If they do so it will be because we haven't used our biological knowledge, but instead have employed chemists as our hired assassins to kill our fellow creatures in their caveman fashion, ignorantly, wantonly, wastefully. There *are* ways of dealing with our insect enemies, as the biologists are continually pointing out. The most sensible and obvious way is to cherish and encourage *their* enemies. For instance, you can provide nesting boxes in forests for beneficial birds; you can introduce new predators from abroad; you can wage war with specific bacteria and fungi which affect only a particular species or group of species, and so constitute a much more accurate weapon against your enemy than the spray which blots out large populations of your friends. *Know your enemy* is a good slogan in any kind of war: know how he lives, what are his habits, needs, frailties, where he is most vulnerable. Only the biologists can provide the answers. Chemists are no more than capable executioners; sensible men employ judges and juries, and not executioners, to decide whom they must hang.

As it happens, Alfie Perks on his market-garden is faced with a classic example of a pest having increased as a direct result of our chemical warfare against it. For many years he and his fellow gardeners all over Britain have sprayed their sprouts and cabbages and cauliflowers with various D.D.T. preparations in order to kill the caterpillars of the large white and small white cabbage butterflies. The chief natural enemy to these caterpillars is an ichneumon fly called *Apanteles glomeratus*. It is a small deadly thing: so small that a hundred of its larvae can sustain themselves upon the living body of one caterpillar, in which they have hatched from eggs laid beneath the caterpillar's skin by the parent ichneumon. They carefully avoid the vital organs; their host must be kept alive as long as they require him! Then, when he is about to change into a chrysalis, they eat their way out of him. He dies; and the *Apanteles* larvae spin a cluster of yellow cocoons around whatever may be left of him.

Since the parasite inevitably lives most of its life in close association with the host, our D.D.T., directed at the caterpillars, must kill *Apanteles* also. So it has done, for years. But the cabbage butterflies, every autumn, renew their populations through mass-immigration from abroad. *Apanteles* has no immigrants to sustain it. The butterflies lay their eggs on the cabbages, and the resulting caterpillars have a high old time, because there are few if any *Apanteles* left to attack them.

This year we have had a sudden, large incursion of large whites. (They fly over, helped by a friendly breeze, from France, and gradually disperse themselves over the country.) 'Never sin so many butterflies,' says Alfie ruefully. 'Never sin so many blasted grubs, either.' He sprays, of course; again and again, expensively both in material and in labour; all the same half his cauliflowers are spoiled. He understands the fallacy behind what he is doing. 'We've killed off our pals, and now we're by ourselves against our enemies.' But chemical warfare is a sort of treadmill: once you engage in it you've got to go on.

'Your father didn't have to spend all this money on sprays,' I say.

'That he didn't or he'd 'a' bin bloody broke.'

'Your grandfather had never heard of such things.'

'O' course he hadn't.'

'But he grew good cauliflowers, I dare say?'

'Yes. They'd 'a pick the grubs off by hand, mos' likely, little boys and girls, when labour was chip. And the birds helped, and those pals of ours that lays the yellow eggs' – he meant the yellow cocoons of *Apanteles*, of course. 'But it's all very well for you to talk. You ain't a gardener. You don't grow things for your living. We've killed our pals, I agree; so we'll never be *able* to stop spraying, whatever happens, will us?'

What if the spray against the cabbage whites one day ceases to work? No *Apanteles*; possibly – the way we're going on – not very many birds; and those smelly greeny-yellowy caterpillars immune to our chemistry?

Who'll win then?

Alfie's under no illusions.

'The bloody grubs,' says he.

The Year of the Pigeons

~

The tragic writings of Jefferies are almost entirely concerned with himself; whereas Hudson, looking down from his eagle height, saw the whole of Nature, the inter-relation of genera and families, the slow, inevitable crawl of the evolutionary process, culminating in the tragedy of Man. One of the greatest benefits conferred by a scientific education is the consequent realization of one's own comparative unimportance; Hudson could find no tragedy in his own affairs; but he could write majestically of the tragic passing of a whole beautiful species:

'And, above all others, we should protect and hold sacred those types, Nature's masterpieces, which are first singled out for destruction on account of their size, or splendour, or rarity, and that false, detestable glory which is accorded to their most successful slayers. In ancient times the spirit of life shone brightest in these; and, when others that shared the earth with them were taken by death, they were left, being more worthy of perpetuation. Like immortal flowers they have drifted down to us on the ocean of time, and their strangeness and beauty bring to our imaginations a dream and a picture of that unknown world, immeasurably far removed, where man was not: and when they perish, something of gladness goes out from Nature, and the sunshine loses something of its brightness.'

Man was but another species to Hudson; and if this strange mammalian should go the way of the trilobite and the dinosaur in the fullness of evolutionary time – well, he could contemplate the prospect of its passing with no more regret than he felt for the passing of the great auk. After all, it could not match for beauty the rippling swiftness of a snake, the poise of a young gazelle, the delicacy of a humming-bird, the splendour of a lion; and if it had wisdom which none other possessed, if it could tame the fire and the winds and the waters to its purposes, if it could number the stars in the heavens and comprehend the infinite distances of interstellar space, if it could write the tragedies of *Hamlet* and *Macbeth* and *Lear* – what was the use, since that wisdom was employed also to destroy Nature's loveliest and rarest creatures, and to invent the pole-trap, and to cage a white owl till it pined away and died?

Country Men

WEATHER

~

With hey, ho, the wind and the rain

SHAKESPEARE

I do not know if, as children, we were brought up to be unusually preoccupied with the wind and the weather. Perhaps we were . . . One of my earliest memories is that of being warned solemnly by our Nanny that, should we persist in pulling childish faces, looking sulky, or being tearful, 'the wind would change' and we would remain thus for the rest of our lives. A quelling thought, which doubtless had a salutary effect, and caused an immediate change of countenance.

Then there were such rhymes as 'Red sky in the morning, shepherds' warning. Red sky at night, shepherds' delight,' which I can remember knowing as long as I can remember anything, and which was a forecast that proved surprisingly accurate. Less accurate, but believed to be true – perhaps because it was learned from the 'Grown-ups' – was the theory that, should it rain on St Swithin's Day (July 15th) it would rain for forty days thereafter. 'When the wind is in the East, 'tis neither good for man nor beast' was a couplet which froze the blood, and was another tenet of our weather creed.

Small wonder, then, that John grew up to be almost obsessed by the weather, as can be seen in his book, *The Season of the Year*.

This new, unsullied Naturalist's Diary of mine has weather-rhymes printed in it, about half a dozen for each month. All are characterized by a spirit of dark foreboding.

> The blackest month of all the year
> Is the month of Janiveer,

strikes the authentic ominous note at the head of page one; but lest the anonymous poetaster should prove mistaken for once in a way, and gentle days should lift my flagging spirits towards the spring, he has another couplet up his sleeve:

> If the grass grows in Janiveer
> It grows the wuss for it all the year.

Indeed he can go on in this strain for as long as anybody is prepared to listen to him:

> If Janiveer Kalends be summerly gay
> 'Twill be wintery weather to the Kalends of May.

I hate this rustic Homer, who is I suppose the compound and quintessence of innumerable old country crotchets rolled into one lump of misery. I see him as crooked, crabbed, toothless, rheumy, intolerably loquacious, an inescapable bore at warm inn-hearth or bitterly cold street-corner, always bellyaching about something, about the Government, about the laxity of the times, about the Young People and their Morals, the Children and their Indiscipline, the speed of motor-bikes, the Things they say in the Newspapers, the Woes of the World. I'll rhyme him an answer:

> *If it snows or shines in Janiveer*
> *May he never enjoy his beer.*

So much for old January Screwnose. Of course, regarding the blackest month, he is quite often right. According to the old records, people skated on our local rivers, the Severn and the Avon, during January in 1795, 1814, 1820, 1821, 1838, 1846, 1854, 1861, 1871, 1881, 1891 and 1895. That was the Great Frost, when it began freezing at Christmas and went on till March. I can remember my father telling me how they roasted an ox on the Severn right in the middle of the stream. The local paper set up a printing-press on the ice and printed a special edition. There was pride in my father's voice as he told me these things, as if to imply: My boy, we were tough chaps in those days!

Countrymen love extremes of weather: at least they love to remember them afterwards. A great frost, a deep snow, a high flood, a mighty rushing wind: I think that Man, who always has at the back of his mind a very proper awareness of the huge power of the elements, and always has a sneaking suspicion that they could freeze him stiff, bury him under the snow, drown him or even blow him away if they really set themselves to do so – I think that Man always feels a bit of a hero for simply surviving these extremes. 'My goodness it was a sharp one last night, twenty degrees on my thermometer.' 'The flood came right up to my garden gate.' 'The snow was so deep I had to dig myself out along the garden path.' 'Blow? Lord, I thought it was going to flatten the house!'

I myself can remember the Severn being frozen over – in 1917. As a small boy I went for a walk on it; but I wondered less at the hardness of the frost than at the spectacle of a middle-aged lady called Emily Creese who was very notable for religious works pirouetting on skates like a two-year-old. That this grave and godly woman should be able to skate – should permit herself to skate – and what's more should do figures of eight in a long black skirt which swept the ice – caused me astonishment and awe. That's all I remember about the Great Frost of 1917; but I'm still curiously proud to have walked on the ice across the River Severn.

Another curious thing about our attitude to the weather is that we all as we get older contrive to persuade ourselves that it was never so hot or so cold, so snowy or so blowy, as it was in the days of our youth. François Villon, back in 1450 or so, wrote a ballad with the lovely refrain: 'But where are the snows of yesteryear?' That is the old man's question, always; and I can imagine my father's father, in 1895, saying Tush, boy, this is nothing to what we had in '57; and so all the way back to my great-great-grandfather remembering the frost of 1776, which Gilbert White wrote of in *The Natural History of Selborne*. He called it *'Siberian weather'*, with the countryside looking like Lapland, 'the roads filled above the tops of the hedges, through which the snow was driven into romantic and grotesque shapes, so striking to the imagination as not to be seen without wonder.' He speaks of the strange long silence unbroken by the sound of carriage wheels or horses' hoofs: 'Strange but not pleasant, it seemed to convey an uncomfortable sense of desolation, *Ipse silentia terrent.*' I think the very greatest cold generally has this frightening quality of silence. Coleridge wrote:

> *The frost performs its secret ministry*
> *Unhelped by any wind.*

There's a wonderfully chilly quality about those lines, you can almost feel the silent frost creeping about you. I've been trying to think which are the *coldest* pieces of poetry I know. They both come from Keats who with his ravaged lungs and wasted body probably knew more about cold than most of us. There are those two desolate lines from *La Belle Dame Sans Merci*:

> *The sedge is withered from the lake*
> *And no birds sing.*

All winter, surely, in those eleven words! And then there's the soul-shramming beginning of *The Eve of Saint Agnes*:

> *St Agnes' Eve – Ah bitter chill it was!*
> *The owl, for all his feathers, was a-cold;*
> *The hare limp'd trembling through the frozen grass,*
> *And silent was the flock in woolly fold.*

Keats noticed – only poets and naturalists notice such things – that sheep in great frosts are silent. They do not bleat. They cough now and then, and that hoarse old-man's cough seems to make the silence deeper.

Now when *I* am an old man, of course the weather I shall talk about will be that of February and March 1947. Having recently finished fighting a World War, it seemed specially hard that we should become engaged in a real battle with the elements. And it *was* a battle. That snow *could* kill. In the Welsh mountains it killed a dozen or more people and thousands of sheep. I went out one night – only half a mile, down to the village – and I encountered, on an exposed stretch of the road, the sort of driven snow which I'd always thought of as a film-producer's property: snow blowing sideways like a solid wall, so that it was like a barrier, and when I pushed my way into it I was lost in a white blurr of snow. There were only about 20 yards of it; then I got in the lee of the trees. But as I fought my way through those 20 yards I had an inkling, for the first time, of what Scott and his men suffered as they dragged themselves and the laden sledges through such a blizzard all day long, and for weeks on end. It also occurred to me, a very astonishing and rare thing in our gentle climate, that a sick man or a drunken man could go down and die in that snow. Indeed that night some sick men and some drunken men, in various parts of England, did falter, and go down, and die. My thermometer at home showed -2 degrees Fahrenheit: that is to say 34 degrees below freezing. We took the bread and groceries round the outlying parts of the village on sledges: and that was a queer thing, in England. The bitter spell finished with a gale that blew off scores of chimney-pots, and blew down twenty great elms within a few hundred yards of my house, and then there was a thaw, and the flood was the highest since 1894.

All that I shall tell the young people, if they dare to mention to me frost, snow, flood or wind, subsequent to 1960.

But it's rare in England for the weather really to show its teeth to us. Even Dickens, who made a speciality of writing about winter weather, always speaks of it kindly, as if it were a friendly or at any rate a tameable thing. His fog is 'like beer'. The snow and the hail are like philanthropists, 'coming down handsomely'. You don't get anywhere in Dickens the despairing and desolate feeling that 'the whole world's sap is sunk'. John Donne wrote that, in the reign of the first Elizabeth. 'The whole world's sap is sunk.' It was exactly how I felt in 1947.

The Season of the Year

Being their own weather prophets, the old men naturally mistrust, resent and sneer at the forecasts on the wireless. The forecasters, they hold, are townsmen; and as townsmen they obviously can't know anything about weather. They hate them for being right about the continuing cold. They hate the towny voice of the announcer who has the job of reading the forecast, which of course they believe to be of his own concocting. They became very angry – as indeed we all do – about centigrade.

One thing which the freeze-up has surely taught us is the asininity of trying to impose the centigrade scale against their wishes upon an obstinate and individualist people, such as we English are. For once in a way we were *all* – townsmen as well as countrymen – passionately interested in the weather, and personally concerned with the temperature. There was therefore an unrivalled opportunity to teach us to get used to centigrade, if we were ever likely to do so; but what happened? We were irritated and muddled by it, and we clung on to our old familiar Fahrenheit as devotedly as if it were a tenet of our faith. We didn't learn to think in terms of centigrade, and indeed it was exposed as a very confusing, inadequate and imprecise scale for describing our English temperatures. For example, when we are told that the temperature is expected to be 33°F or 30°F we are in no doubt whatever whether or not a frost is being forecast. But if the announcer informs us that the temperature will be 1°C it may mean either 1°C above or below. He has to tell us which, or to add a plus or a minus.

The damsilly idea seems to be that if the Air Ministry goes on for long enough giving its forecasts in both Fahrenheit and centigrade, we shall become so familiar with the latter that we can be weaned away from Fahrenheit. I suspect a tiresome intellectual arrogance at work over this; and I wonder how well these bureaucrats know us. I still believe that in the long run the sheer inspired obstinacy of ordinary Englishmen will win.

The Year of the Pigeons

O western wind, cried a poet[1] from his heart

> *O Western Wind, when wilt thou blow*
> *That the small rain down can rain?*
> *Christ, that my love were in my arms*
> *And I in my bed again!*

The relevance of the second wish to his general theme isn't crystal clear, but I am with him over the small rain. Today it came in upon a strong steady blow in which even we inlanders could suppose we smelt the Atlantic; and it broke the long spring drought – which is a rare thing with us, for where I live we are a people much rained upon. We may sometimes think we get more wet than is our share; but what good farmer would not rather have a flood than a drought? A flood after all is simply an over-generosity on the part of Providence; a drought is something mean, arid and niggardly as the soul of a Chancellor of the Exchequer. As for the west wind, it bears no resemblance to the soul-shramming, liver-shrivelling blast that comes off the North Sea. It is rough, but with the roughness of a Welsh rugger scrum; it buffets hard but without malice; and there is a hint of wildness in it which finds a response in the adventurous heart. 'Of a' the airts the wind can blaw I dearly love the west,' wrote Burns; and so do we all, even a depressing character I knew long ago who is still remembered among us as The Man Who Shot the Fox. He had persuaded the blacksmith to make him a weather-fox instead of a weather-cock, which he erected over his stables; it was a fine dashing one, carrying its brush straight out behind it and pointing its nose into the wind. If a real fox did so the hounds would soon catch him!

Now one dry spring such as this has been, the old curmudgeon who owned the weather-fox bored us all with his dreary complaints about his liver. 'It's the weather,' he said, 'it's this blessed east wind.' He would come down to the local and lecture us: 'I don't know what's happening to this country. When *I* was a young man the prevailing wind was west; but now it's in the east all the time. I believe it's all those wireless-waves have upset it.' – This was in the time of sound radio; today he'd have blamed television, or hydrogen bombs.

---

[1] Early 16th century? and anonymous.

We put up with him for weeks (because it *was* a rather cold spring, with occasional north-easters) but one very balmy day in April we had to point out to him that by the church weather-cock the wind was due west, and the temperature was sixty degrees, and the bees were humming. 'West?' he said. 'Not it. It hasn't changed since mid-March. I looked at my fox this morning –'

We told him to look again.

He went home and looked at it, and sure enough it was pointing due east. He wetted his finger and held it up in the air. Due west! Then he went indoors to fetch his gun. His family thought perhaps he was going to shoot himself because of his discovery that his 'liver' was nothing to do with the weather after all; but instead he shot the fox. He peppered its brush well and truly (you can see the holes to this day) and he spun it round so that it became unstuck, and ever since then it has told the direction of the wind correctly. However, the old curmudgeon became known throughout the district as the Man Who Shot the Fox; and the nickname clung to him, so that at last even the M.F.H. got to hear of it and, believing that he'd shot a real fox, never asked him to his annual cocktail party again.

The weather-rhymesters, old miseries to a man, have naturally let themselves go about the east wind –

> *When the wind is in the east*
> *The fisherman likes it the least, etc.* –

but I recently came across a rhyme which reprobates all winds equally and so is typical of the countryman's attitude that all weather is bad but some is worse than the rest:

> *Northwind brings hail,*
> *Southwind brings rain,*
> *East winds we bewail,*
> *West winds blow amain.*

And so round the compass like a crazy weather-cock:

> *North-east wind is too cold,*
> *South-east wind is not warm,*
> *North-west wind is far too bold,*
> *South-west wind doth no harm.*

Man and Bird and Beast

EPILOGUE

John was an ardent believer in the concept of the Jack of all Trades – a term invented, incidentally, in the 18th century, though we shall never know by whom! – and in two of his books he enumerates some of the 'many things' he determined to add to his repertoire, even when he was a small boy.

In *The Boys' Country Book* (a little-known work, but one which should be read, marked, and learned by every country boy) he wrote several chapters and edited the whole. Other chapters were contributed by various celebrities of the time, of whom, sadly, few remain today. John concluded the book with an epilogue which affirms much the same view as that contained in the two paragraphs from *The Season of the Year* which I have included below, and I think that all are worth reading, if only to show his immense love of life and his eagerness to experience every aspect of living. This is how he expressed it.

'I know a man who has taken part, at some time or another, in almost every one of the sports and pastimes we have discussed in these 350-odd pages; he's never been really good at any of them, but he's hunted, sailed, climbed, flown, fished, shot, bird-watched, bug-hunted, botanised, collected this and that, taught himself a very little about this and that, read a great deal about this and that, and enjoyed himself so much that he hasn't the slightest regret that none of his boyhood ambitions have been achieved. These boyhood ambitions were: to play cricket for the county (but as it turned out he plays only for the village, with a batting average as a rule of about six); to win the Grand National (but the only time he ever rode in a race he fell off); and of course to become the world's greatest living expert on Hawkmoths, Wild Geese, Orchids or whatever it was that had tickled his fancy and aroused his special interest at any given time. Instead of this he became an incorrigible dabbler with a smattering of knowledge about Hawkmoths, Wild Geese, Orchids and a good many other things, but expert in absolutely nothing.

'I am that man; and although I am sure that you most rightly and properly possess the kind of ambitions I used to have (and what's more may actually achieve them) I want to finish this book by giving you another ambition, which is *to have a shot at doing as many different things as a full life allows you to*. If you achieve this one, let alone any of the others, you'll have a lot of fun out of life; and you'll never be bored, which incidentally is one of the Deadly Sins and sounds much worse in Latin, being called *accidia*.'

This, then was John's challenging philosophy, and in *The Season of the Year*, though the list is different and the aspirations more modest (and largely fulfilled) the philosophy is the same, namely, to live life to the full. This ambition John most definitely achieved . . .

I have always believed that it is a virtue in itself – apart from any practical considerations – to be able to do as many things as possible. When I was quite a small boy I counted up all the possible methods of progression other than shanks' pony and determined that I must learn to ride a bicycle, a motor cycle and a horse, drive a car, row and sail a boat, paddle a canoe, manage a punt, swim and fly. So also with games: I have played, with unbelievable incompetence, every game I can think of including polo, ice-hockey, lacrosse and pelota, with the single exception of croquet, which I am reserving for my later years. I don't think it matters how badly one does these things; it is fun attempting them.

In the same way I think a countryman should at any rate try his hand at all the ordinary jobs and crafts of the countryside. If he owns an orchard with some tall trees in it he should learn how to handle a 30-rung ladder; he ought to have a shot at laying a hedge, at ploughing with a tractor, at felling a tree. For all these things, besides being fun, are in some mysterious way good for the soul.

The Season of the Year